ONE STOP FINANCE

The One Stop Series

Series editor: David Martin, FCIS, FIPD, FCB
Buddenbrook Consultancy

A series of practical, user-friendly yet authoritative titles designed to provide a one stop guide to key topics in business administration.

Other books in the series to date include:

David Martin	*One Stop Company Secretary*
David Martin	*One Stop Personnel*
Jeremy Stranks	*One Stop Health and Safety*
John Wyborn	*One Stop Contracts*

1997 titles:

David Martin	*One Stop Property*
Robert Leach	*One Stop Payroll*
Karen Huntingford	*One Stop Insurance*
David Martin/ John Wyborn	*One Stop Negotiation*
Robin Ellison	*One Stop Pensions*

ONE STOP
Finance

HARRIS ROSENBERG

ICSA Publishing
The Official Publishing Company of
The Institute of Chartered Secretaries and Administrators

in association with

Prentice Hall
London New York Toronto Sydney Tokyo Singapore
Madrid Mexico City Munich Paris

First published 1997 by
ICSA Publishing Limited
Campus 400, Maylands Avenue
Hemel Hempstead
Hertfordshire, HP2 7EZ

Typeset in 10/12.5 pt Meridien with Frutiger Light
by Hart McLeod, Cambridge

Printed and bound in Great Britain by
T. J. International Ltd.

British Library Cataloguing in Publication Data
A catalogue record for this book is available from
the British Library

ISBN: 1–86072032–3

1 2 3 4 5 01 00 99 98 97

Acknowledgements

We would like to thank the many people who have advised and helped us
in the course of preparing this book.

Particular thanks must be given to Harvey Spillman, for the many hours
he spent reviewing, amending and constructively criticising the draft
manuscript, to Paul Kleinman and Maurice Moses for their technical
guidance, to Sue Carter for typing this book and to Michelle Rosenberg for
proof-reading.

We are also very grateful to Hereward Philips (Chartered Accountants)
for supplying the specimen business plan included in the annex.

Contributors:
G. M. Baird, European Investment Bank; Patrick Berry; David Freeman;
Paul J. Hodgson-Jones, ECGD; David Horowitz; Howard Lewis; Charlotte
Morrison, BVCA; Peter Monument, Barclays Bank Plc; Carole Moscisker;
Peter Musgrave; Andrew Ross; Jenny Scott, Fishburn Hedges; James Ward;
Keith Williams, British Steel (Industry) Limited; Lauren Wolman; Mitchell
Wrightman.

Contents

Part 3 Model business plan

Preface

Whenever an individual opens or expands a business, many types of finance have to be obtained. The forms of finance available to businesses vary greatly. Each has its implications, advantageous or otherwise, and its costs. In the case of loans, for example, the costs would generally take the form of a negotiation fee and the interest payable. However, even a personal cash injection is not without cost. Using money for one purpose means it is not, or will not, be available for something else. In such cases the costs could be considerable: loss of interest; loss of flexibility; reduction in collateral.

Frequently, the terms used by grantors or lenders are unfamiliar to those seeking finance at the early stages of their business. Part One will deal with terms you may come across in your objective of raising finance. It does not attempt to be an exhaustive account of current accounting procedures and practice, but aims to provide a guide to common accounting terms.

Whereas you may know instinctively whether or not you have sufficient money to cover your costs, a financier, or bank manager, from whom you may wish to obtain money, will not have this insight. They will analyse the financial implications of proposals to assess the level and price of help they will provide. An understanding of such terms will therefore enable you both to consider and to prepare the course of action required to obtain their – often invaluable – help.

The ease with which these many forms of finance can be obtained is often dependent upon you giving the impression that you know what you are doing. Few lenders or grantors are likely to give or lend money to an organisation on the basis of trust. Part Two provides a summary of the most common forms of finance that may be required in order to establish and develop a business. It will look at the most common forms of finance available to small and medium-sized businesses. This will include information how to obtain government and other grants for which you may be eligible. Some of these will not, owing to their very nature, be available. For example, certain grants are location sensitive; venture capital is often inappropriate if only small sums – for example, a few thousand pounds – are required. Other forms of finance, for example, bank loans, may be suitable whatever the size of your business or its financial requirements. Invariably, several of the forms of finance mentioned will be used.

It is hoped that this book will prove itself to be a user-friendly guide enabling you to evaluate your own needs as well as understand the considerations of those from whom you will be seeking help.

Harris S. Rosenberg
BA (Hons), DMS, MCIM, MIMng
May 1997

The need for finance

What causes the need for finance? In simple terms, finance is needed either to cover existing costs or to provide money for future expenses. It may be obtained either from existing or from new resources. Obtaining funding for short-term needs is often not difficult providing you have:

(a) money available

(b) the ability to more than cover projected expenditure.

In general, eight stages will cover the raising of project finance:

1. What is my project?
2. Project formulation
3. Preliminary financial considerations
4. Project review
5. Project financing
6. Approaching sources of finance
7. Will more than one type of finance need to be considered?
8. Implementation and review

1. What is my project?

It is important that you clearly define your project – ideally by giving it a title – upon which to peg requests for support.

You must remember that money is generally given for a reason. A project title should enable you to reply to the question 'What do you want the money for?'

2. Project formulation

Having ideas is only part of the process involved. These ideas have to be converted into reality by action. People and organisations putting money into a project need to be not only inspired by them but also comfortable that the project has a chance of succeeding. A written business plan will almost certainly be helpful.

Initial steps

Preparing a business plan need not be complex. Indeed, a concise and relevant business plan is often preferred by lenders. The information required will normally include some background details such as:

(a) a description of the business
(b) management and staffing
(c) market information
(d) existing and potential customers
(e) competition
(f) finance.

Am I able to, or should I, undertake my proposed project?

A SWOT (strengths, weaknesses, opportunities, threats) analysis of each of the factors mentioned in (a)–(f) above will help you to assess your organisation prior to project implementation.

Tying project to business plan

Having considered your business you can now look at it in relation to your proposed project. Whilst a book of this nature cannot tell you whether you will succeed or not, it may at least help you to reflect upon your project in the same way as any financial institution or backer. All projects involve risks. Undertaking homework in the form of a preliminary business plan should at least identify these.

3. Preliminary financial considerations

Undertaking a project, no matter how small, not only involves a reallocation of resources, including time and money, but also requires you to determine the potential sales of any product or service, and the price for which it can be sold. Equally, you will need to consider the costs of establishing the project, including any ongoing manufacturing and staffing costs relating to it. In all cases you need to be prudent.

Having established, hopefully, that the product or service is capable of being provided at a price that will attract customers, you can then look at the financial resources available. The range of these is wide and many are referred to throughout this book.

After making these assumptions you should then be able to prepare both a budget and a cashflow.

Budget

A BUDGET will identify in advance all income and expenditure leading to a given project objective. A budget may be drafted on the basis of the total project period or staged, for example, on a three-month basis. Budget headings will usually reflect items stated in an organisation's cashflow.

Cashflow forecast

A cashflow will look at the income and expenditure relating to a project at the time when money is expected to be received or spent. In most project situations, there will be little income derived at the early stages as there will be few products or results of service to be paid for. Conversely, expenditure will be required to create the product or service to be sold. It is at this stage that finance needs to be injected into an organisation. Where income is derived from a lender, the lender will want a return for this based upon both the sum loaned and the perceived risk.

4. Project review

Having drawn up a preliminary business plan, you would be wise to undertake further research and to test assumptions made in respect of a proposed project. Visits to shops, a review of telephone directories, and discussions with a few potential customers will help. Research will also enable you to test assumptions about costs and credit terms given by suppliers, as well as the price you will be able to command from potential customers. In undertaking market research you may discover opportunities to be maximised and identify risks to be minimised or avoided. Lastly, at this stage, you would determine the price of premises and machinery needed.

5. Project financing

Having more precise information on costs and credit terms offered will enable you to determine and to prove assumptions made in any budgets and cashflows. Should your earlier assumptions prove erroneous you would be able, at this stage, to pull away from a project that might prove to be costly. Equally, should your assumptions prove conservative, you will be able to embark upon the project with greater confidence.

Often, an entrepreneur will produce not only the basic cashflow but a sensitivity cashflow. A sensitivity cashflow is one in which certain factors are changed either downwards or upwards. For example, you may wish to look at the effect of reducing the potential sales by 10% to see the effect on the financial requirements of the business. Equally, sensitivity cashflows can be used to determine finance needed by moving assumed income.

Figure 1 Example of a cashflow forecast

	JAN	FEB	MAR	APR	MAY	JUN	JUL	AUG	SEP	OCT	NOV	DEC	TOTAL
INCOME													
Sales													
Commissions													
Royalties													
Equity													
Loans (bank)													
Loans (other)													
Grants													
Other income													
VAT													
Total													
EXPENDITURE													
Materials													
Directors' salaries													
Wages													
PAYE													
Commissions													
Royalty payments													
Pension scheme													
Rent													
Rates													
Gas													
Electricity													
Service charges													
Plant repairs													
Property maintenance													
Insurance													
Carriage													
Packing													
Telephone													
Postage													
Printing													
Stationery													
Motor expenses													
Other travel expenses													
Business accommodation & subsistence													
Advertising/promotion													
Entertainment													
Recruitment													
Training													
Research & development													
Consultancy													
Computer Expenses													
Sundry expenses													
Legal													
Accountancy													
Audit													
Other professional fees													
Lease payments													
Bank charges													
Bank interest													
Capital expenditure													
Corporate tax													
VAT													
Total													
Surplus (deficit)													
Opening bank balance													
Closing bank balance													

Figure 2 Extract taken from a completed cashflow forecast

	JAN	FEB	MAR	APR	MAY	JUN	JUL	AUG	SEP	OCT	NOV	DEC	TOTAL
INCOME													
Sales	80000	80000	50000	50000	50000	40000	40000	40000	200000	100000	80000	80000	890000
+VAT@17.5% (Note 1)	14000	14000	8750	8750	8750	7000	7000	7000	35000	17500	14000	14000	155750
Total	94000	94000	58750	58750	58750	47000	47000	47000	235000	117500	94000	94000	1045750
EXPENDITURE													
Materials	30000	30000	40000	30000	30000	30000	30000	20000	20000	30000	30000	30000	350000
Directors' salaries	3000	3000	3000	3000	3000	3000	3000	3000	3000	3000	3000	3000	36000
Wages	9000	10000	10000	10000	10000	10000	10000	10000	8000	8000	9000	9000	113000
PAYE	4000	4200	4200	4200	4200	4200	4200	4200	3700	3700	4000	4000	48800
Commissions	4000	4000	2500	2500	2500	2000	2000	3000	10000	5000	4000	4000	45500
Royalty payments	2000	2000	1250	1250	1250	1000	1000	1500	5000	2500	2000	2000	22750
Pension scheme	450	450	450	450	450	450	450	450	450	450	450	450	5400
Rent	0	0	9000	0	0	9000	0	0	9000	0	0	9000	36000
Rates	0	0	3000	3000	3000	3000	3000	3000	3000	3000	3000	3000	30000
HP/Lease payments	600	600	600	600	600	600	600	600	600	600	600	600	7200
Bank charges	0	0	250	0	0	250	0	0	250	0	0	250	1000
Bank interest	0	0	-4000	0	0	300	0	0	4300	0	0	-3400	-2800
Capital expenditure	0	20000	25000	0	500	500	0	0	0	10000	0	0	56000
Corporate tax	0	0	0	0	8000	0	0	0	0	0	0	0	8000
VAT (Note 1)	6940	9967	13586	6577	6394	6779	6005	4649	6754	8588	6934	7333	90507
Total	68045	89622	120621	68362	75079	78714	63970	55864	88099	81863	71009	79588	940837
Surplus (deficit)	25955	4378	-61871	-9612	-16329	-31714	-16970	-8864	146901	35637	22991	14412	104914
Opening bank balance	25000	50955	55333	-6538	-16150	-32479	-64193	-81163	-90027	56874	92511	115502	105628
Closing bank balance	50955	55333	-6538	-16150	-32479	-64193	-81163	-90027	56874	92511	115502	129914	210541

The company has an agreed overdraft facility of £1,000,000.   Note 1: VAT would be paid quarterly in arrears. However it is prudent to make provision for this on a monthly basis.

5

6. Approaching sources of finance

Should internal finance be inadequate, you will need to identify and seek other sources. The steps taken to determine the amount of finance required will enable you to present a professional approach to any lender. Only rarely can an entrepreneur obtain finance from unknown, or even known, sources on the strength of an unconsidered proposal. Nothing annoys lenders or grantors more than the businessman or woman who, at the stage of asking for money, only just begins to work out how much is needed.

An acronym used by some financiers prior to lending any money is PAPERS:

Purpose   – the reason for the request for finance

Amount   – the sum required

People   – the character and track record of the lender

Enough   – has the sum requested been carefully calculated? Is the project financially sound?

Repayments – can the applicant maintain capital and interest repayments to the lender and pay any capital sum at the end of the term?

Security   – what collateral is the applicant prepared to offer for financial support given?

A professionally presented proposal will not only demonstrate that you are serious about the project, but will also provide a basis for sensible discussion on the financial needs of the project.

7. Will more than one type of finance need to be considered?

Often project finance will comprise several elements ranging from an immediate cash injection to short-, medium- and long-term finance.

Example

XYZ Limited, a clothing manufacturer, wishes to buy a freehold building for £150,000. In addition, £50,000 will need to be spent on building costs to make the site appropriate for clothing manufacture. Equipment and machinery costing £100,000 and two vehicles costing £25,000 will also be required. The project will be financed as shown in the table below.

Amount	Nature of finance	Purpose	Repayment period
£20,000	Lease purchase for vehicles		Medium term
£75,000	Hire purchase for plant and machinery		Medium term
£90,000	Mortgage	Building	Long term
£35,000	Cash injection	General	Long term
£25,000	Overdraft	General	Short term
£20,000	Director's loan	General	Medium term
£75,000	Bank loan	Building and general	Medium term
£15,000	Cashflow (profit)	General	Short term

An example such as the one quoted above, whilst demonstrating a variety of financial methods of funding a project, does not take account of advantageous forms of finance, for example, government grants. It also does not account for the repayment periods for the help sought. For example, a bank loan payable over a longer period will require smaller regular payments even though the total sum ultimately paid will be greater.

Where larger projects are involved it is often useful to seek professional advice, not only to discuss the forms of finance sought but also the tax implications relating to them.

8. Implementation and review

On the assumption that finance is available for the project it would be up to you to implement your project. Frequent review is necessary. In the early days this would be to ensure that your project is not only reaching the targets hoped for, but also that a tight rein is kept on the funding of the business. Many businesses founder through not taking adequate care of their financial health at this early stage.

Constant review will enable you to both prove and amend your original forecasts. Hopefully the changes will be positive, resulting from better than anticipated sales, or inflow of income. Equally, if targets are not being met, early action will enable you to address this problem or even, if necessary, to mitigate any losses by ending your project.

Model set of accounts

Many of the terms referred to within this section are identifiable in the accounts of most organisations. To assist the reader the following model set of financial statements of a limited company is included. The accounts of a sole trader or partnership will differ in style although their purpose will be the same.

The company accounts used are those of a limited company that is a retailer engaging in a small proportion of own manufacturing. Only pertinent information has been taken in order to demonstrate financial terms that are to be found in the text that follows.

Whilst the amount of detail shown will vary from company to company, either on the basis of style or statutory requirement, the accounts which are being used will represent those common throughout the United Kingdom.

It should be appreciated that disclosure requirements for limited companies will differ according to a number of factors including turnover, net assets and average number of employees.

The notes referred to by numbers on the left-hand side of the page are those from within the set of accounts themselves. The terms are defined in detail in the alphabetical listing that follows this section.

Model Retailer Limited

Profit and loss account
For the year ended 31 MAY 1997

	Note	1997 £	1996 £
Turnover	10	480,339	426,989
Cost of sales	11	(291,493)	(254,892)
Gross profit		188,846	172,097
Net operating expenses			
Distribution costs	13	(67,605)	(64,989)
Administrative expenses	14	(86,989)	(90,217)
Other operating income	12	2,600	9,200
Operating profit	2	36,852	26,091
Interest payable	15	(10,348)	(10,345)
Profit on ordinary activities before taxation		26,504	15,746
Taxation on ordinary activities	3	(13,691)	(6,663)
Profit on ordinary activities after taxation		12,813	9,083
Dividends		(8,000)	(10,000)
Retained profit/(loss) for the year	9	4,813	(917)

Continuing operations
None of the company's activities was acquired or discontinued during the above two financial years.

Statement of total recognised gains and losses
There were no recognised gains and losses in the above two financial years other than the results for the year and, accordingly, no statement of total recognised gains and losses has been prepared.

Balance sheet at 31 May 1997

	Note	£	1997 £	£	1996 £
Fixed assets					
Intangible assets	4		32,000		32,000
Tangible assets	5		17,307		24,976
			49,307		56,976
Current assets					
Stocks		235,400		237,100	
Debtors	6	760		–	
Cash at bank and in hand		3,289		–	
		239,449		237,100	
Creditors					
amounts falling due within one year	7	(273,369)		(283,502)	
Net current liabilities			(33,920)		(46,402)
Total assets less current liabilities			15,387		10,574
Capital and reserves					
Called up share capital	8		2		2
Profit and loss account	9		15,385		10,572
Equity shareholders' funds			15,387		10,574

The directors have taken advantage in the preparation of these financial statements of special exemptions provided by Part I of Schedule 8 to the Companies Act 1985 on the basis that the company qualifies as a small company.

The financial statements on pages 7 to 10 were approved by the board of directors on 3 June 1997.

Chairman

Notes on financial statements

31 May 1997

1. Accounting policies

Basis of accounting

The financial statements have been prepared under the historical cost accounting rules.

The company has taken advantage of the exemption from preparing a cash flow statement conferred by Financial Reporting Standard No. 1 on the grounds that it is entitled to the exemptions available in Section 246 to 247 of the Companies Act 1985 for small companies.

Depreciation

Depreciation of fixed assets is calculated to write off their cost or valuation less any residual value over their estimated useful lives as follows:

Leasehold land and buildings   over period of leases
Plant and machinery   10%
Fixtures and fittings   10%

Stocks

Stocks are valued at the lower of cost and net realisable value. Cost is computed on a first in first out basis. Net realisable value is based on estimated selling price less the estimated cost of disposal.

2. Operating profit

	1997 £	1996 £
Operating profit is stated after crediting		
Net rental income (Note 12)	2,600	9,200
	====	====
and after charging		
Auditors' remuneration (Note 13)	1,100	1,100
Operating leases		
Hire of assets other than plant and machinery		
(Note 13)	7,716	3,440
	====	====
Depreciation of tangible fixed assets (note 5)		
owned assets	7,669	7,821
	====	====

3. *Tax on ordinary activities*

	1997 £	1996 £
Corporation tax on profit on ordinary activities at 24%	6,500	–
Advance corporation taxation	2,000	2,500
Interest on corporation tax	2,271	–
	10,771	2,500
Under provision in earlier years	2,920	4,163
	13,691	6,663

4. *Intangible fixed assets*

	Trademark £
Cost	
1 June 1996 and 31 May 1997	32,000
Amortisation	
June 1996 and 31 May 1997	–
Net book amount	
31 May 1997	32,000
1 June 1996	32,000

5. Tangible fixed assets

	Plant and Machinery	Fixtures and Fittings	Land and Building	Total
Cost £	£	£	£	
1 June 1996	3,712	23,436	35,728	62,876
31 May 1997	3,712	23,436	35,728	62,876
Depreciation				
1 June 1996	1,875	11,545	24,480	37,900
Charge for year	184	1,189	6,296	7,669
31 May 1997	2,059	12,734	30,776	45,569
Net book amount				
31 May 1997	1,653	10,702	4,952	17,307
1 June 1996	1,837	11,891	11,248	24,976

6. Debtors

	1996 £	1995 £
Amounts falling due within one year		
Other debtors	760	–
	760	–

7. Creditors

Amounts falling due within one year

	1996 £	1995 £
Bank overdraft	88,001	81,456
Trade creditors	62,736	92,026
Other creditors	122,632	110,020
	273,369	283,502

The bank overdraft is secured by the personal guarantees of the directors.

8. Called up share capital

Equity share capital	Number of shares	£	Number of shares	£
Authorised				
Authorised share capital @ £1 each	10,000	10,000	10,000	10,000
	=====	=====	=====	=====
Allotted called up and fully paid @ £1 each	2	2	2	2
	=====	=====	=====	=====

9. Profit and loss account

	1997 £	1996 £
Retained profit/(loss) for the year	4,813	(917)
Retained profit brought forward 01 June 1996	10,574	11,491
Retained profit carried forward at 31 May 1997	15,387	10,574

	1997		1996	
	£	£	£	£
10. Turnover				
Sales		480,339		426,989
All turnover was generated from continuing operations				

11. Cost of sales				
Opening raw material stock	6,300		8,600	
Opening stock of finished goods	230,800		206,747	
Purchases	289,793		276,645	
Closing raw material stock	(4,200)		(6,300)	
Closing stock of finished goods	(231,200)		(230,800)	
		291,493		254,892
Gross profit		188,846		172,097

15

12. Other operating income

Net rental income		2,600	9,200
		———	———
		191,446	181,297
Distribution costs	67,605		64,989
Administrative expenses	86,989		90,217
Interest payable	10,348		10,345
	———		———
		164,942	165,551
		———	———
Net profit for the year		26,504	15,746
		======	======

Directors and employees

Staff costs:			
Directors' remuneration			
for the year	20,400		20,400
	———		———
Wages and salaries	19,908		20,700
Social security costs	2,295		2,334
Other pension costs	3,120		2,400
	———		———
	25,323		25,434
	=====		=====

There were four employees during the year apart from the directors (1996 = four employees).

(The following is for the information of the Directors only and does not form part of the statutory financial statements.)

Schedule to the trading and profit and loss account for the year ended 31 May 1997

	1997 £	1996 £
13. Distribution costs		
Salaries and wages	19,908	20,700
National Insurance	2,295	2,334
Advertising	1,590	198
Hotel and overnight expenses	396	–
Motor expenses transport and travel	5,511	8,529
Directors' car allowance	4,000	4,000
Telephone and telecommunications	2,489	2,686
Printing postage and stationery	180	302
Vehicle leasing	7,716	3,440
Directors' remuneration	20,400	20,400
Directors' pension costs	3,120	2,400
	67,605	64,989
	=====	=====
14. Administrative expenses		
Heating and lighting	3,078	3,804
Repairs and renewals	1,210	3,982
Insurances	223	94
Rent and rates	49,389	50,547
Sundry expenses	1,887	940
Bank charges	2,791	4,750
Finance charges	4,308	3,759
Professional fees	15,334	13,420
Auditors' remuneration	1,100	1,100
Depreciation short leasehold	6,296	6,296
Depreciation plant and equipment	184	204
Depreciation fixtures and fittings	1,189	1,321
	86,989	90,217
	=====	=====
15. Interest payable		
Bank interest	10,348	10,345
	10,348	10,345
	=====	=====

17

PART 1
Financial terms

Accounting period

Limited companies

An *accounting period* is the period elected by an organisation to be the duration of its *financial year*. Companies registered before 1.4.96 were required to nominate a date on which their first accounts would be made up – an accounting reference date (ARD). For companies registered after that date their ARD is initially fixed as the last day of the month in which their anniversary of incorporation falls. Thus their first 'accounting period' will be 12 months (plus possibly a few weeks).

An ARD can be changed (which has the effect of altering the length of the accounting period) although (with some exceptions) a company cannot extend its accounting period within 5 years of a previous extension. Generally an accounting period can be shortened without restrictions.

At the end of this *accounting period* a trading and profit and loss account is prepared showing the trading position of the organisation for that period. A balance sheet will also be drawn up showing the organisation's financial position as at that particular date.

In the United Kingdom the accounting period (subject to the above) is discretionary, although in some countries, for example, Spain, a set date of 31 December is mandatory.

Accounting periods are described as *for the year ended*, or *for the period from — to —*. Corporation tax will usually be based upon that period's adjusted profits as taxation on profits is based on a paid/received basis whereas the accounting profit is based on the accruals concept.

Sole traders and partnerships

Like limited companies, the accounting period of sole traders and partnerships will normally run for a period of 12 months. However, the choice of year end is at the discretion of the owner or partners. This may be changed freely.

Common principles

Accounts drawn for the year end are historic, i.e. they show the position of a company at a date that may be several months previous. As a result, management accounts are often required by lenders or grant providers should the audited or company accounts be more than six months old.

Accounts

Audited accounts are the financial statements drawn for an organisation upon which an independent auditor states his opinion as to whether or not those financial statements show a true and fair view of its profit or loss and state of affairs as at the end of its financial year and whether they have been prepared in accordance with the Companies Act 1985. Drafted on a concept that a company is a *going concern*, they aim to state the net assets of a business at a particular moment in time, rather than what the business may be worth to a potential purchaser (see GOODWILL).

Financial accounts

Financial accounts are prepared in order to meet reporting requirements, e.g., a limited company reaching its year end. They relate to specific organisations or a group of organisations. They might be audited if required to be so. A potential investor, for example, may ask for this before injecting a capital sum.

Management accounts

Management accounts are prepared by a business, on a going concern basis, to judge its performance for a period and for it to see its net assets position. These accounts are not necessarily prepared according to external reporting requirements, i.e, they may be prepared according to the management's needs. They are not usually audited. Such accounts are often requested by investors, lenders or grantors should audited or financial accounts be more than six months old.

Audited accounts

Audited accounts will generally comprise:

(a) the company's annual accounts, including a balance sheet, profit and loss account, cashflow statements* and notes to the accounts

*The cashflow statement submitted for accounts demonstrates how cash resources have been increased or reduced during the year, i.e. it is not a cashflow forecast.

(b) the directors' report for the financial year

(c) the auditors' report on those accounts.

The auditor signing the accounts in the vast majority of instances will be a chartered or certified accountant authorised to carry out audits. Sole traders do not require an audit but may find it prudent to obtain professional advice.

Companies that qualify as small with gross assets not more than £1.4 million, and have an annual turnover not exceeding £90,000, are not required to have an audit. (The directors are still required to prepare and file true and fair accounts.)

Companies that qualify as small (gross assets not more that £1.4 million) and have an annual turnover over £90,000 but not over £350,000, can have an Accountant's Report instead of an audit. However, for accounting periods ending after 22 June 1997, this has been abolished and all companies with an annual turnover not exceeding £350,000 are no longer required to have an audit.

In both situations, holders of 10% of the shares can demand an audit. Certain companies, such as insurance companies, are required to have an audit, irrespective of their turnover.

All limited companies must file their accounts at Companies House where they are available to the general public. The amount of information required to be included in these accounts will vary according to the size of the company, i.e., the smaller the company the fewer the details that need to be revealed. Shareholders are still entitled to receive a full set of financial statements. These may also be requested by institutions, such as a bank. In these circumstances, a small limited company is defined as one that meets two of the following three attributes:

1. turnover less than £2.8 million
2. gross assets less than £1.4 million
3. fewer than 50 employees.

Accruals

Accruals, which are a *current liability*, (see LIABILITIES), are sometimes referred to as 'accrued liabilities'. An accrual is an amount that, at the end of a financial period, has not been invoiced but where the liability to pay the amount exists. Such sums should be accounted for as a current liability to the organisation. Examples of accruals include:

(a) salaries
(b) wages
(c) royalties
(d) commissions
(e) goods received but not yet invoiced
(f) services rendered but not yet invoiced
(g) credit card payments, for example, for petrol
(h) PAYE
(i) pension provisions
(j) interest
(k) HP and lease payments
(l) rates
(m) rent.

Accrued liabilities will normally be paid in the following financial period. If the amount actually paid differs from the amount accrued, for example, because it was estimated, an adjustment will be made at that time.

Certain liabilities, for example, VAT, are not considered as accruals as they relate to sums due and are accounted for as an outstanding debt. Such sums may be separately identified within current liabilities.

Added value

Added value is the value added to the purchases of a company by the labour of its employees.

Certain grant applications, for example, the Department of Trade and Industry's application form for the grant of Regional Selective Assistance, specifically require this information. The formula to calculate added value per employee is:

$$\frac{\text{Sales} - \text{purchases}}{\text{Number of employees}} = \text{added value per employee.}$$

Amortisation

Amortisation refers to the process by which an asset or a liability is written off over a period of time. The term is synonymous with DEPRECIATION, and is usually used when writing down the value of an asset with a finite life, for example, a leasehold property.

Amortisation may also be used when writing off intangible assets (see ASSETS), goodwill, patents or copyrights.

A formula used to calculate amortisation is:

$$\frac{\text{Cost of asset}}{\text{Expected life (number of years)}} = \text{£ per annum.}$$

The formula above does not account for any estimated residual value. This may be taken from the cost of the asset.

Generally, where the values concerned are small, a company will write off the value of that purchase in the current accounting period. However, where the sums concerned are large, amortisation will be used in order to allocate part of the cost of the asset over each year of its economic or actual life, whichever is the shorter.

Assets

An asset is a right or item, *intangible* or *tangible*, capable of bringing benefit to a company. Where it has a monetary value, this sum will be accounted for in the company's BALANCE SHEET.

Assets are resources owned by an organisation, accounting for their book value as at a particular moment in time.

One of the greatest resources of a business, its staff, is not regarded as an asset for accounting purposes. Definitions, however, do change from time to time, an example being the asset value of a professional footballer. Since the Bosman ruling, a footballer's contract is no longer regarded as a business asset, and the registration fee is written off at the time of signing.

Assets are, for accounting purposes, generally defined as:

(a) tangible
(b) intangible.

Any assets may be defined as fixed or CURRENT.

Tangible fixed assets

These are items which have a permanence within the business. They are usually categorised as:

(a) land and buildings
(b) plant and machinery
(c) tools and equipment
(d) fixtures and fittings
(e) motor vehicles.

Tangible assets may be worth more or less than their BALANCE SHEET value, depending upon obsolescence, changing money values and market trends. Assets other than land will generally be anticipated as having a decreasing worth over a period of time and their value will be depreciated (see DEPRECIATION) to reflect this.

Example

Model Retailer Limited has over a number of years, purchased fixed assets with an original cost of £62,876. Through DEPRECIATION, those assets now have a book value of £17,307.

Tangible fixed assets

	Plant and Machinery	Fixtures and Fittings	Land and Building	Total
Cost	£	£	£	£
1 June 1996	3,712	23,436	35,728	62,876
31 May 1997	3,712	23,436	35,728	62,876
Depreciation				
1 June 1996	1,875	11,545	24,480	37,900
Charge for year	184	1,189	6,296	7,669
31 May 1997	2,059	12,734	30,776	45,569
Net book amount				
31 May 1997	1,653	10,702	4,952	17,307
1 June 1996	1,837	11,891	11,248	24,976

Examples of tangible fixed asset

Capital equipment is the term used to define plant and machinery. Such equipment is regarded as an asset to the company. Its book value, nevertheless, will be written down over an accepted period of years to account for wear and tear and obsolescence (see DEPRECIATION). Consumable items such as lubricants are not regarded as capital equipment.

Fixtures and fittings are assets that may be 'fixed' or 'fitted' to the fabric of a building. Heating, lighting and plumbing appliances may fall within this definition as they are capable of being separately identified and, although unlikely, could be removed from the fabric of a building.

Raising finance for any of these items may determine how they are treated, e.g. with mortgage finance generally being cheaper than hire purchase, a borrower may prefer the cost of a heating system to be included in the value of a building.

Intangible assets

Intangible assets, often referred to as *intangible fixed assets*, are resources which have acquired their value as a result of expenditure. Even a trademark will have had some expenditure defrayed, e.g. the cost of labour and professional advice. The value reflected in accounts, however, may not be the same as the amount that would be realised on its sale.

Intangible assets may be divided into three groups:

(a) those assets with a limited life, for example, patents, copyrights

(b) those assets with an unlimited life, for example, goodwill, brand names and trade marks

(c) development costs, providing the reason is justifiable.

Patents and copyrights, unless renewed, have a decreasing value as the protection they offer a company is limited to a period of time. Equally, patents may become of decreased value as new products, performing similar functions, appear on the market, e.g. a patent held on a gramophone record would, for example, be of decreasing value owing to the advent of tape cassettes and compact discs.

Intangible assets with an unlimited life do not have a finite period over which they may be written down. Prudence should always be taken in valuing such items.

Audit

An audit is a process in which independent persons, who are usually chartered or certified accountants, will review a company's financial position as at a certain date, usually being the end of the organisation's financial year or accounting period (see ACCOUNTS).

Auditors will be required to follow methodical procedures in assessing the financial worth of a company. To do this they will collect, collate and interpret evidence leading to their assessment. These methods are outlined in professional auditing standards and guidelines recognised by the Institute of Chartered Accountants in England and Wales, the Institute of Chartered Accountants in Ireland, the Institute of Chartered Accountants in Scotland and the Chartered Association of Certified Accountants.

When conducting an audit, the auditor will aim to produce an opinion, based upon his work and the evidence that he has collected, as to whether or not the accounts, for which the directors have sole responsibility in preparing, show a *true and fair* view of:

(a) the state of affairs as at a particular point in time (usually the end of an accounting period)

(b) its profit or loss for the period ended on that date.

Smaller companies, not having the expertise available to produce the accounts themselves, often engage the services of their auditor to undertake this task as well. It should, however, be noted that the auditor carries out this assignment quite separately from that of his audit.

Auditors will take a prudent view with regard to the value of items such as work in progress and of plant, machinery, vehicles and other assets that have a depreciating value.

Example

A company manufactures men's trousers. As at the end of its financial year there was a considerable stock of semi-finished garments. The value of those trousers, for auditing purposes, would not be the full value of the manufactured trousers but a lesser value reflecting little more than the value of cloth and trimmings used. An auditor would have to consider carefully the value of partially made goods on the basis of the company being a going concern.

Bad debts

A *bad debt* reflects sums that a business is unable or unlikely to receive. Bad debts arise due to:

(a) debtor becoming insolvent

(b) a debtor refusing to acknowledge a liability and no legal claim being possible

(c) an amount ignored as a gesture of goodwill

(d) an amount not claimed owing to the inconvenience and possible costs involved to the debtor.

Bad debts will be *written off* in a company's PROFIT AND LOSS ACCOUNT.

Where the incidence of bad debts is frequent, a company may make a provision for doubtful debts. Such a provision will be reflected in the profit and loss account by entering an amount equating to:

(a) a percentage of the year's total sales
(b) a percentage of the year end trade debtors
(c) a calculation of total doubtful debtors.

Where a company has paid value added tax on the value of sales, the tax defrayed may be reclaimed providing the bad debt is acknowledged by an insolvency practitioner.

Balance sheet

A *balance sheet* is a statement defining, in monetary terms, the cost or value of assets, liabilities and shareholders' funds 'at' a particular date. The amounts given should show a true and fair view of the state of affairs of a company as at that particular date.

A balance sheet will always be drawn to show an organisation's financial affairs being in a state of equality showing amounts owed to, or by, the owners. The formula often used is:

Assets – liabilities = owner's equity.

Example

Using figures from Model Retailer Limited's balance sheet (page 11)

Fixed assets + current assets – creditors = allotted share capital + retained profit

(£49,307 + £239,449 – £273,369) = £2 + £15,385

The formula does not suggest in any way the financial strength or otherwise of the company.

Often investors, or grant-awarding bodies, will wish to know the value of assets in a business to determine whether or not there is sufficient collateral in the organisation to attract and retain investors. The value of a company's assets, at the end of its financial year, less total creditors, is referred to as a *balance sheet total*.

Break-even points

The *break-even point* reflects the financial state at which total costs equal revenue.

In calculating the break-even point all factors remain the same, for example, the price of goods or services may change. It is always, therefore, prudent to allow for a margin of safety when making this calculation. Several formulas are used to calculate the break-even point.

Break-even point of sales

The break-even point of sales =

$$\frac{\text{fixed costs}}{\text{fixed costs + maximum net profit}} \times \text{maximum sales.}$$

The maximums are assumed when calculating forward a break-even point of sales.

Break-even point of production output

The break-even point of production =

$$\frac{\text{fixed costs}}{\text{unit selling price – unit variable costs}} = \text{units produced.}$$

Break-even point of production capacity

The break-even point of production capacity =

$$\frac{\text{total production capacity – break-even point}}{\text{total production capacity}} \times 100.$$

Budget

A budget is a financial and quantitative statement, made prior to a defined period of time, of a policy to be pursued in order to obtain one or more given objectives. As such, budgets should be used to direct future events rather than correct past errors – (see BUDGETARY CONTROL).

Budgets may be drawn on a short-term basis which typically would be:

(a) three months or six months where short lead times are required to manufacture, supply and arrange payment for goods

(b) 12 months for established businesses

(c) several years where a large-scale investment is proposed, for example, building a steel mill.

Items included in the budget will be similar to those identified in a cashflow statement.

Budgetary control

Budgetary control is a technique used by businesses for:

(a) planning
(b) control.

Budgetary control tends to look at short-term situations, falling within the overall financial plans of the business. Where there are discrepancies in a budget these are called *variances*. Where the variance is not favourable action must be undertaken to correct it.

Budgetary control aims to identify clearly costs directly attributable to a project. It will consider financial implications including:

(a) the amount of any lending facility
(b) its cost
(c) terms of repayment
(d) duration during the *budgetary period*.

To be effective, budgetary control needs to be undertaken by one or more individuals. Ideally, responsibility will be in one person's hands.

Business plan

A business plan is a statement outlining an organisation's business objectives and how they are to be achieved. Business plans are not drafted in isolation and will make reference to past and present factors. Business plans will always include financial information and projections, including budgets and cashflow forecasts.

Business plans vary according to the needs of the business. They will generally contain information as is shown in the sample business plan in Part Three.

Capital

Capital is the amount that may be owed to the owners or investors in the business. It usually reflects the cash injection brought about by the issue of shares in a company.

The *capital structure* of a company will be defined by the nature of investment in the company. This may comprise a mix of different forms of shares, including ordinary shares, non-participating preference shares and loan capital.

Cash

Cash is an amount comprising money readily available to a company from its own resources. It is sometimes referred to as *liquid assets*. It includes:

(a) currency (cash in hand)

(b) bank balances

(c) cheques paid into an account

(d) money orders

(e) monetary instruments capable of conversion readily into currency or able to be converted into a bank balance at short notice (less than three months).

Cash does not include shares or investments in other organisations, even if they are capable of conversion into cash at short notice.

Cashflow forecast

A cashflow forecast is a statement that refers to expected income received and expenditure defrayed as at the date of the transfer of funds. The cashflow statement should disclose separately, where material, individual categories for items, for example, rent, wages, etc. An example of the cashflow forecast is given on pages 4 and 5.

An appreciation of cashflow is a critical factor in determining whether a business can survive. Inadequate finance to undertake or continue its business may lead a company to its demise.

Devising a cashflow will help you to predict the cash needs of your business thereby pre-determining any situation that could cause a business failure. Inadequate funds to match the business you are currently undertaking or anticipating is known as OVERTRADING.

When large sums are involved, or where prediction is difficult owing to the number of unknown factors, it may be prudent to provide a sensitivity cashflow. A sensitivity cashflow will vary one or more factors stated in the master cashflow. As the sensitivity cashflow is aimed at prudence, the factors will be adverse. Typical changes that may be considered include:

(a) reducing turnover by a small percentage

(b) increasing the length of payment from debtors

(c) increasing the sums payable to creditors

(d) including a contingency amount to reflect unexpected expenditure, for example, a price increase.

A sensitivity cashflow will normally be presented alongside the principal cashflow statement. Both will be used to determine a funding facility required.

Collateral

Collateral is the *security* required by a lender to mitigate its risk. The collateral requested, or offered, may be a direct transfer, a charge or second charge over an asset (usually a property) or by way of a guarantee.

The provision of collateral would not necessarily prevent the applicant having access to and use of the assets, for example, a factory may be used as collateral for a business loan.

Costs

Costs incurred by a business fall into two categories:

(a) direct costs
(b) indirect costs.

Direct costs

Direct costs are the amounts that will need to be, or have been spent, in undertaking a specific project. Direct costs will comprise *variable costs* and *fixed costs*.

Example 1

The direct costs to a manufacturer would be the raw materials, specific components and labour costs directly attributable to the manufactured item.

Example 2

The direct costs for a retailer would be goods he offers for sale. The cost of shop assistants, rather than supervisory staff, may also be considered a direct cost.

Example 3

The direct costs attributable to a service industry would include terms that can be specifically identified for a particular customer or client. Travel expenses are an example. Other expenses which are small and not directly attributable to a project, are not usually allocated in this way owing to the time and effort involved.

An analysis of specific and relevant costs of a project may be determined by BUDGETARY CONTROL techniques.

Indirect, fixed or overhead costs

Indirect costs are those that are not directly attributable to the production process and are incurred as a general expense in running your business or managing your project.

Indirect costs fall into two categories:

(a) fixed overheads: these are amounts which remain constant over a period of time but which may, in the long term, be variable, e.g. rent, rates, hire purchase and other finance costs.

(b) general overheads: these are often not attributable to any specific part of the business and vary according to the amount used, e.g. heat, lighting, travel, telephone calls, printing, postage and stationery.

It is usual to consider directors' or partners' salaries and drawings as indirect costs.

Credit and debit entries

Credit

A *credit* is an amount stating an indebtedness to another party. The person or company that is owed this sum is called a CREDITOR.

Debit

A *debit* is an amount stating the sum owed to you by another party. The person or company that owes this sum is called a DEBTOR.

Credit and debit entries are recorded through the process of DOUBLE ENTRY BOOKEEPING.

Credit entries include:
(a) the disposal of an asset
(b) the reduction in value of an asset
(c) receipt of revenue
(d) acknowledgement of a liability
(e) the introduction of capital by shareholders
(f) reduction of expenses, e.g. issue of credit notes.

A credit entry will always be associated and balanced with a *debit entry*.

Debit entries include:
(a) receipt of an asset
(b) acknowledgement that an asset is to be received
(c) losses
(d) the extinguishing of a liability
(e) the withdrawal of capital or profits by shareholders or owners.

Example

Where money is spent on goods (credit) it would expect to receive those goods in exchange (debit).

Person 1	Person 2
Pays money (credit)	Passes over goods (debit)
Receives goods (debit)	Receives money (credit)

Creditor(s)

A *creditor* is an individual or organisation to whom money is owed in respect of goods or services delivered or to whom a monetary commitment is due. The term *creditors* refers to the groups of individuals or organisations to whom money is owed. They are sometimes referred to as *accounts payable*. Creditors may be *short term* or *long term*.

Short-term creditors

Short-term creditors are organisations to whom money will be payable within the period of 12 months (see LIABILITIES). Amounts under the heading short-term creditors often include:

(a) trade creditors, i.e. organisations or individuals to whom a debt is owed for goods provided or services rendered

(b) accruals, i.e. amounts owed but not yet invoiced

(c) PAYE

(d) bank overdraft and short-term loans.

Long-term creditors

Long-term creditors are organisations to whom payment would not be due for over 12 months. Examples of long-term creditors include:

(a) debenture holders
(b) long-term loans
(e) hire purchase companies.

Should a business operation fall into difficulties certain creditors will take preference with regard to payment from any existing funds (*preferential creditors*). These include Her Majesty's Customs & Excise (VAT), the Inland Revenue, the company's bankers, organisations administering or handling the company's affairs should it be in receivership, administration or liquidation and debenture holders. Creditors would then be entitled to their claim prior to preferential and ordinary shareholders.

Current assets

Current assets are those assets which are either already cash or can reasonably be expected to be converted to cash within 12 months from the end of a company's financial year. Most liquid assets (or cash) would be regarded as current assets.

Investments and other *monetary assets* in a company, for example, stocks and shares, may also be regarded as current assets but would be separately categorised.

In a set of accounts, current assets may include:

(a) cash at bank and in hand

(b) trade debtors – the individual or organisations who owe you money

(c) prepayments – amounts paid in advance relating to goods or services to be provided after the accounting date

(d) other debtors – money owed from other sources, e.g. some governmental funding

(e) stock or *inventory*, i.e. goods available for sale

(f) agreed grant claims payable

(g) work in progress

(h) promissory notes.

Items such as these are sometimes called '*circulating assets*' as they continually change over a period of time.

Debentures

A *debenture* is a form of loan which is sometimes secured by a charge on assets of a business. Although a debenture is placed on distinct items, debentures are sometimes referred to as *charges*. Types of debenture include:

(a) *fixed debenture*, which is usually secured on plant and machinery

(b) *mortgage debenture*, which is secured upon property

(c) *floating debenture*, which is a charge attached to the general assets of a business.

Debentures provide the debenture holder (usually a bank) with control over a particular asset until the debenture is discharged. A company cannot dispose of the assets without the permission of the debenture holder. Where the debenture is held on a secured charge, the debenture holder will take preference over other creditors.

Debtor(s)

A *debtor* is an individual or organisation who owes you money in respect of goods or services supplied or amounts due from other transactions. Debtors in the former category are often referred to as trade debtors, and sometimes as *accounts receivable*. Cash retailers are unlikely to have many debtors as most of their sales are paid for at the time of purchase.

In a company's set of accounts, debtors would include:

(a) trade debtors

(b) other debtors

(c) prepayments and other specified assets

(d) factored debtors outstanding

(e) legal or insurance claims that have not yet been paid

(f) tax that is recoverable.

Debtors should be reduced to account for doubtful or BAD DEBTS.

Debtors due after a period of 12 months must be disclosed by way of note to the accounts.

Depreciation

On the basis that a capital asset will have a useful life for only a finite period of time, it is common practice to write down the value of that asset, that is, depreciate its value. *Depreciation* therefore reflects the fall in value of an asset caused by age, wear and tear, obsolescence caused by market or technological changes and saleability. Freehold land is not usually depreciated, although *depletion* may be a consideration. Buildings may be depreciated, but this would be over a long period. The deduction in value is reflected in a company's PROFIT AND LOSS ACCOUNT.

In a BALANCE SHEET, depreciation is deducted from the cost of an asset to give a *net book value*. It should be noted that the *book value* of an asset is not necessarily its market value. As such, the depreciated value of an asset does not reflect its current purchase price or its price if it were to be sold.

Should any asset suffer a permanent reduction in value in excess of the amount of depreciation for that period, for example, because of obsolescence, the excess amount should be written off the book value of the asset and future depreciation charges reappraised if necessary. Equally, if a value increases, the financial presentation of the asset may be altered accordingly. Such situations are rare.

The three principal methods of depreciation are:

(a) straight line method
(b) reducing balancing method
(c) depletion.

Straight line depreciation

The formula used for straight line depreciation is:

$$\frac{\text{Original cost} - \text{residual or scrap value}}{\text{estimated life of asset}} = \text{depreciation per annum.}$$

Example

G purchases a computer and printer for £2,100. G estimates that the computer will have a useful life of four years before it becomes obsolete.

49

At the end of that period G may be able to part-exchange it for £100. Using the above formula:

$$\frac{£2100 - £100}{4} = £500$$

The depreciation per annum will therefore be £500.

Reducing balancing method

This method recognises that not all assets depreciate at an even rate. The formula used for this method is:

Year 1   Cost x depreciation rate (%) = net book value, end of year 1

Year 2   Net book value (end of year 1) x depreciation rate (%) = net book value, end of year 2.

and so on.

Depreciation rates often used are:

(a) 10% for plant
(b) 25% for machinery, fixtures and fittings
(c) 25% for vehicles
(d) 33.33% for computers.

Example

H buys a vehicle for £12,000, which is depreciated at 25% per annum. At the end of the first year the vehicle will have a net book value of £12,000 – 25% = £9,000. In the second year the vehicle will have a net book value of £9,000 – 25% = £6,750. This process will continue until the asset is sold.

Depletion

Depletion relates to wasting assets such as mines or quarries. In this situation the asset's life is estimated in terms of its output rather than years. In such cases depreciation is calculated per unit of output, for example, for every tonne of coal sold.

Dividends

Dividends are a method of giving a monetary return to shareholders for their investment in an organisation.

Payment of dividends is governed by the articles of a company. They can only be paid if there are distributable reserves. These factors will allow the directors to determine whether or not a dividend should be paid, and how much it should be. Shareholders can approve, reject or reduce the proposed dividend, but not increase it. If no dividend is recommended, the audited accounts should state 'the directors do not recommend payment of a dividend'.

Payment of dividends

Dividends may be paid periodically through a company's financial year. An interim dividend will often state the sum the directors are prepared to pay in total for the financial year. For payment of interim dividends, directors do not need shareholders' approval. A *final dividend*, for which shareholder approval is needed, would be proposed at the company's year end, and paid some time after. This is referred to as a *proposed dividend*.

In companies where the directors hold either all or a substantial number of shares, dividends may be taken as part of the total remuneration package as they could be a tax-effective way of receiving remuneration.

The dividends are regarded as the top slice of the shareholder's income. If he/she is liable to pay income tax at the lower or basic rate only, no further tax would be due on the dividends. This leaves, therefore, the lower or basic rate bands available for other income.

Double entry bookkeeping

Double entry bookkeeping is the method by which transactions are recorded to ensure that total debits always equal total credits.

For every transaction two entries will be recorded. There will be a *debit* posting and a *credit* posting.

A debit posting account will be for the value of an asset acquired, a liability reduced or an expense incurred.

A credit posting account will be for the value of a liability incurred, an asset reduced or income received.

Traditionally, *debit entries* are recorded on the left and credit entries on the right in a two-sided set of accounts (see CREDIT AND DEBIT ENTRIES).

The principle of double entry bookkeeping is perhaps best explained by use of an example.

Example

If J buys a computer for £1,000 cash, two events occur:

1)   J gains a computer

2)   J loses £1,000 in cash.

Double entry transactions are recorded in accounts to reflect these events. The purchaser's transactions are recorded as follows:

Example

Computer Account	Cash Account
Cash £1,000	Computer £1,000
This reflects the value of the computer coming into the business.	This reflects the cash going out of the business on purchasing the computer.

Balances on accounts relating to income or costs will form the profit and loss account. Balances on accounts relating to assets or liabilities will form the balance sheet. At the end of every accounting year, balances on the former group of accounts will be transferred to a balance sheet account (known as retained reserves or simply as the profit and loss account) and will start again, at nil, for the new accounting period.

Exceptional items

Exceptional items are those which are noticeable owing to either their infrequency or the significance of their size or incidence.

Exceptional items include:

(a) profits or losses on the sale or termination of an operation

(b) the cost of reorganising, restructuring and integrating a business purchased

(c) reorganisation and restructuring costs within the existing company

(d) profits or losses of the disposal of fixed assets

(e) the sale of part of a business

(f) sums defrayed in purchasing a brand name

(g) the input of a large sum of money from an unusual source, e.g. an insurance claim

(h) the receipt or payment of sums resulting from legal proceedings.

Gearing and long-term solvency ratios

Gearing is sometimes referred to as 'capital gearing' or *leverage*. Gearing outlines the relationship between funds provided to a company by individuals or organisations providing short-term and long-term finance. Since the level of risk taken by those providing long-term finance is lower, the return that is given for use of capital will be smaller. Sources of long-term finance include unsecured loans, debentures and preference shares. Conversely, for short-term finance, where this risk is greater, lenders of short-term money will, not unreasonably, require a greater reward.

Where an organisation has high levels of debt relative to its short-term financial base, then a high proportion of income generated will be used to service the debt.

The objective of long-term solvency ratios is to enable a lender or investor to assess the applicant's ability to meet its long-term commitments.

Long-term solvency ratios include:

(a) debt to equity ratios

(b) times interest earned ratio.

Debt to equity ratios

These include:

$$\frac{\text{Debt}}{\text{Equity}}$$

or

$$\frac{\text{Short long-term financial liabilities}}{\text{Shareholders' funds}}$$

or

$$\frac{\text{Long-term loans + preference shares}}{\text{Ordinary shareholders' funds}}$$

55

A company's capital structure is *highly geared* if fixed charges need to be serviced by an above-average proportion of the company's income. The above ratios will show the relationship of debt to equity. The larger the ratio, the less protection there is for lenders. Companies with a strong asset base tend to be lower geared owing to their reduced dependence on invested capital.

Another formula used is the *total debt to equity ratio*:

$$\frac{\text{Current liabilities} + \text{long-term debt}}{\text{Shareholders' equity}}$$

None of the ratios cited above consider collateral or guarantees held against the given debt.

Times interest earned ratios

Two further ways of looking at gearing are through *times interest earned ratios*. These are:

$$\frac{\text{Profit before interest and tax}}{\text{interest (gross)}}$$

or

$$\frac{\text{Income before interest}}{\text{Periodic interest charges}}$$

These formulae, whilst useful, should not be adhered to slavishly as they ignore the existence of reserves. For example, many analysts add book reserves in shareholders' funds.

Goodwill

Goodwill is the difference between the sum paid for an organisation less its net assets, or where an asset is acquired for a sum in excess of that represented by identifiable value.

Goodwill will reflect perceived and often unmeasurable qualities of a business including business contacts, market outlets, historic reputation, exclusivity, development potential, access to production and location.

Insolvency, liquidation and bankruptcy

Insolvency

Insolvency occurs in either of the following situations:

(a) when a company's or an individual's total debts exceed total assets, or

(b) when a company or an individual is unable to pay debts when they fall due.

Where the insolvency is of a personal nature, the individual, if unable to repay his debts, is declared *bankrupt*. Companies cannot become bankrupt. Directors who continue to run a company while knowing it to be insolvent may not be able to hide behind the veil of limited liability and may be personally liable to the company's creditors.

Insolvency may be avoided by a number of methods including:

(a) rearranging the capital base of a company
(b) injecting new sources of capital
(c) arranging longer payment terms with creditors
(d) restructuring the business.

These can be achieved through formal or informal insolvency procedures, some of which are described below. To prevent insolvency, difficult and unpleasant decisions sometimes have to be made but ultimately decisive action is more likely to succeed than inaction.

The Insolvency Act 1986 stipulates that where a company trades while insolvent and is put into creditors' voluntary liquidation, the court may declare a director personally liable and require him personally to find sums to pay creditors. This is especially true where a director either trades fraudulently, or knew, or should have concluded, that an insolvent liquidation was unavoidable and failed to take steps to minimise the loss to the creditors by continuing to trade (wrongful trading).

Forms of winding up a company include an administration order. This is a court order, under which a company that is, or is likely to become, insolvent is placed under the control of an administrator. The administrator will be an insolvency practitioner. Administration orders are granted following a *petition* by the company, its directors or a creditor to the court. The purpose of the order may be to allow the company to remain in business, thereby allowing a reorganisation to ensure the most advantageous realisation of its assets whilst protecting the company from action by creditors. Section 10 of the Insolvency Act provides the powers to a company to protect it from 'any' precipitous action.

Liquidation

Liquidation is a process whereby a company has its assets sold and the proceeds distributed to pay, where possible, its debts and to repay its shareholders. The term *winding up* is also used. Liquidation is a terminal process and is followed by the dissolution of the company. In many cases, liquidation will follow a company falling into receivership or administration. Forms include:

1. Creditors' Voluntary Liquidation (CVL). The liquidation is commenced by a resolution of the shareholders recognising that their company is unlikely to be able to settle all its liabilities. The CVL will be under the effective control of creditors, who can appoint the liquidator.

2. Members' Voluntary Liquidation (MVL). A Members' Voluntary Liquidation applies to companies that are not insolvent. Under an MVL the shareholders appoint a liquidator to realise assets and settle all its debts all within a 12-month period.

3. Striking off. Under the Deregulation and Contracting Out Act 1994, directors can apply to the Registrar of Companies for the company to be struck off provided a company has not, in the previous three months:

    a   changed its name
    b) traded or conducted business
    c) engaged in any activity other than that connected with this application
    d) made a disposal for value of property rights.

    A court order is needed to reinstate the company.

4. Company Voluntary Arrangement (CVA). A Company Voluntary Arrangement allows a company to reorganise its business affairs in order to satisfy outstanding debts. The plan is put forward to creditors and shareholders. There is minimal involvement by the court with the scheme being under the control of a supervisor who is an insolvency practitioner.

5. Receivership. This term is applied when a person is appointed as an *administrative receiver* or *receiver*. Receivers are appointed by a *secured creditor*, usually a bank, which has a charge, normally fixed or floating, over company assets. The receiver is generally an *insolvency practitioner*, except in rare cases such as under the Law of Property Act. He will normally attempt to continue the business of the company in order to secure payment for secured, preferential creditors and other creditors. Often companies that undergo receivership may be liquidated where goodwill and other assets have been realised.

6. Compulsory liquidation. A creditor applies to court for a petition to wind up a company for non-payment of a debt. The most likely creditors to instigate such action are the Inland Revenue or Her Majesty's Customs & Excise. The Official Receiver, an official of the Department of Trade and Industry, is subsequently appointed by the court to conduct the administration of such an appointment. An insolvency practitioner may subsequently be appointed as liquidator.

Bankruptcy

A bankrupt is an individual against whom a bankruptcy order has been made by the court. The bankruptcy order signifies that an individual is unable to pay his debts and deprives him of his property. This is then sold and the proceeds distributed amongst his creditors. Bankruptcy does not preclude a debtor from negotiating a scheme or voluntary arrangement to ensure the best commercial return to creditors is achieved and to organise an exit from, or annul, a bankruptcy order.

Liabilities

Liabilities are the amounts owed by an organisation to others. They include:

(a) amounts owed to the bank on overdraft facilities used and bank loans

(b) amounts owed to other organisations

(c) amounts owed to creditors.

Amounts owed to the owner of the business are not a liability but generally would be regarded as CAPITAL.

Current liabilities are the amounts owed and payable within the ensuing financial year. ACCRUALS would be regarded as current liabilities.

Net current liability is the difference between current assets and creditors falling due within one year, where creditors exceed current assets.

Example

Model Retailer Limited

Balance Sheet at 31 May 1997

Current Assets	£
Stocks	235,400
Debtors	760
Cash at bank and in hand	3,289
	239,449
Creditors	
Amounts falling due within one year	(273,369)
Net current liabilities	(33,920)

Long-term liabilities include loans, debentures and other creditors payable over more than one year after the end of the accounting period.

Contingent liabilities are liabilities that may *possibly* arise owing to a situation not provided for by insurance, for example, a legal claim. Where contingent liabilities are potentially critical to a business they must be stated in a limited liability company's accounts.

Margin and mark-up

A *margin* is the difference between what a product costs to buy and process to a state where it can be sold, and its sale value. Thus, if a product costs £80 and sells for £100 (ignoring VAT), its margin is £20 or 20% of its selling price.

A *mark-up* or *mark-on* is the amount by which the cost price of a product is increased to reach its sale price. Thus, in the example above, where the margin was 20%, the mark-up is £20, or 25% of the cost price of £80.

Overtrading

Overtrading results from an expansion in sales without the capital base to support the increase in trade. Increases in purchases and a rise in debtors not matched by cash receipts into the business may, unless financial support for an interim period is found, result in the business having insufficient cash to continue trading and failing unless additional finance is sourced.

Payback

The *payback* period is the time taken for an investment in an asset to cover its cost.

Example

The electricity costs of a freezer centre amount to £10,000 per annum. The purchase of capacitors for freezer motors, which would result in 20% less electricity needing to be used, will cost £4,000. On the assumption that electricity prices do not rise, a saving of £2,000 per annum will be achieved. This will equate to a two-year payback period on the purchase of the new equipment.

Payback should not be confused with the BREAK-EVEN POINT which considers the relationship between costs and revenue rather than costs and savings.

Prepayments

Prepayments or *prepaid expenses* are sums paid in advance for use of an asset or a service.

In company accounts they are treated as a current asset as they are sums that 'theoretically' are repayable.

Usual examples of prepayments are:

(a) rent

(b) rates

(c) insurance premiums

(d) subscriptions

(e) other services paid in advance.

Profit

Two forms of profit may be recorded by a company:

(a) gross profit
(b) net profit.

Gross profit

The gross profit of a company is sometimes referred to as its *trading profit*.

The gross profit comprises TURNOVER less the direct cost of goods sold. As such, it will account for opening and closing stock.

Example

The gross profit of Model Retailer Limited for the year ended 31 May 1997 was £188,846.

Trading Account for the year ended 31 May 1997

	£	£
Turnover		
Sales		480,339
Cost of sales		
Opening raw material stock	6,300	
Opening stock of finished goods	230,800	
Purchases	289,793	
Closing raw material stock	(4,200)	
Closing stock of finished goods	(231,200)	
		291,493
Gross profit		188,846

The gross profit is the sum reflected in a company's *trading account* (see PROFIT AND LOSS ACCOUNT).

Net profit

The net profit of a company reflects the gross profit less fixed and general overheads (see COSTS). Apart from these, net profit will also account for:

(a) depreciation
(b) interest on loans
(c) operating lease and rental charges
(d) auditor's remuneration
(e) exceptional items
(f) income from investments
(g) discounts allowed or received
(h) bad debts and provisions
(i) directors' emoluments
(j) directors' or past directors' pensions
(k) compensation payments.

Such a profit is sometimes called an *operating profit* or *surplus*. It reflects the profit on ordinary activities or operations of a company after any finance charges, interest levied and received. Where the total of expenses exceeds the gross profit a *net loss* will be made.

Example

Model Retailer Limited

Profit and Loss Account for the year ended 31 May 1997

	1997
	£
Gross profit	188,846
Net operating expenses	
Distribution costs	(67,605)
Administrative expenses	(86,989)
Other operating income	2,600
Operating profit	36,852

Should a net profit occur, tax may be payable. The sum retained by a business, after accounting for tax to be paid, is called the net profit after taxation.

Example

Model Retailer Limited

	1997
	£
Profit on ordinary activities before taxation	26,504
Taxation	(13,691)
Profit on ordinary activities after taxation	12,813

Profit and loss account (including trading account)

Trading account

A *trading account* details the costs directly involved in manufacturing goods for sale or, in the cases of retailers, purchasing goods for sale, against the income derived from the organisation's own sales to its customers. The trading account will also include opening and closing stocks (see STOCKS). This will produce the gross profit figure, from which all other expenditure incurred and other income received by the company during its accounting period is deducted This will leaving a resulting net profit or loss for that period.

By law, this statement must give a 'true and fair view' of the profit or loss.

Profit and loss account

The *profit and loss account* outlines a company's income and expenditure on non-trading items, and declares the organisation's net profit or loss. By law, this statement must give a 'true and fair view' of the profit or loss.

Items stated in the profit and loss account may be classified in general headings, for example, administration, facilities, financial costs, or be described in greater detail.

The profit after taxation will then be appropriated either by way of payment of dividends etc., or by being transferred to reserves.

Example

MODEL RETAILER LIMITED

<u>Profit and loss account for the year ended 31 May 1997</u>

	1997 £
Trading Account	
Turnover	480,339
Cost of sales	(291,493)
Gross profit	188,846
Profit and Loss Account	
Net operating expenses	
Distribution costs	(67,605)
Administrative expenses	(86,989)
Other operating income	2,600
Operating profit	36,852
Interest payable	(10,348)
Profit on exceptional activities before taxation	26,504
Taxation	(13,691)
Appropriation Account	
Profit on ordinary activities after taxation	12,813
Dividends	(8,000)
Retained profit/(loss) for the year	4,813

Ratio analysis

Shareholders, investors and others seeking to provide financial assistance, to invest in, or to continue to support an organisation will *always* examine the applicant's financial situation with regard to its solvency and performance.

In addition to those wishing to lend money to a business, others such as merchandise suppliers or even customers will examine these figures to ensure that the organisation they wish to deal with will not let them down either in terms of payment, or in ability to supply as a result of a lack of cash.

Whilst '...a favourable ratio may mean nothing... an unfavourable ratio is significant' (S. Gilman), it will always provoke deep questioning of the company's current and future position by any investor, including the company's bankers. An explanation of adverse factors, in the short term, may be acceptable to an investor, however you can be certain that a calculation of the risk involved will be made and additional security may be requested.

Short-term liquidity and solvency

Liquidity or *solvency* ratios are used to determine an organisation's current ability to pay for goods and services either supplied or to be supplied. These ratios are often considered the most important as they will determine whether a company is able to survive. For peace of mind, owners of businesses are advised to look at these particular ratios regularly.

The key ratios are:

(a) acid test or quick ratio
(b) current or working capital ratio
(c) flow-of-funds ratio.

Ratio analysis, particularly in respect of liquidity, is a normal feature of business life and an understanding of these, as well as an appreciation of a CASHFLOW FORECAST are fundamental principles to the survival and potential growth of a business.

Acid test ratio

The acid test or quick ratio is also known as the *liquid ratio*.

The formula representing the acid test ratio is:

$$\text{Acid test ratio} = \frac{\text{cash + readily marketable securities}}{\text{Current liabilities}}$$

The items on the numerator represent sums immediately available to a company. The above formula does not take account of precise times when revenues will be received, nor does it account for the time taken to pay creditors.

Ideally, parity should be sought, i.e. a ratio of 1:1. This, however, would be unusual for certain forms of business, such as retailers and, in itself, may not be a critical factor.

A factor that would be looked at critically is a deterioration in this ratio for this would indicate that debts are not being settled, or alternatively that cash is not being collected.

Current ratio

This ratio defines the amount available to a company to undertake its daily business. It is sometimes represented by the formula:

$$\frac{\text{Current assets}}{\text{Current liabilities}}$$

A 2:1 position will often be sought by lenders or suppliers, although nowadays, 1.5:1 is often considered more 'normal'. Circumstances and industry norms will determine whether this safety margin is appropriate.

The above ratio is sometimes referred to as the *working capital ratio*. This defines the margin of safety in which a firm is operating. It will tell how many times CURRENT ASSETS cover current LIABILITIES. The larger the current ratio, the larger the safety margin of short-term creditors.

Working capital

Working capital is defined by the formula current assets less current liabilities. When this figure is positive it indicates that the company is in a position to finance its medium-term activities.

The working capital requirement for projects is sometimes defined by the formula:

Increase in debtors + increase in stocks – increase in creditors.

The increase in creditors would exclude capital items and charges for hire purchase, finance charges, lease charges, taxation, dividends and overdraft. Lenders would look for increases in working capital of at least 10%.

Flow of funds ratio

The flow of funds ratio looks at the movement of funds to and from a business over a period of time rather than at a static date. The flow of funds ratio is sometimes called the *movement of funds ratio*, or the *sources and uses ratio*, or the *'where got, where gone'* ratio.

Flow of funds ratios can be used to show the solvency of an organisation on a periodic basis. It looks at relationships between cash inflows and outflows throughout a period as well as taking note of existing liquid assets held by a company.

Formulas used to calculate flow of funds ratios include:

$$\frac{\text{Current assets}}{\text{Average daily expenditure}}$$

$$\frac{\text{Net working capital}}{\text{Net earnings + depreciation + other non-cash charges}}$$

$$\frac{\text{Anticipated monthly income}}{\text{Anticipated monthly expenditure}}$$

$$\frac{\text{Sources of all funds}}{\text{Uses of all funds}}$$

Profitability ratios

Profitability ratios are used to evaluate a firm's efficiency in using money invested. They also examine the organisation's ability to generate income in excess of expenditure. With such ratios the numerator defines the factor against which investment is judged, whilst the denominator states the investment base. Ratios used to assess profitability include:

$$\frac{\text{Numerator}}{\text{Denominator}} = \frac{\text{Net income}}{\text{Total assets}} = \text{net income to total assets}$$

This ratio will measure the profitability of an organisation's assets, thereby indicating how efficiently capital is used.

Other asset-based ratios include:

(a) net sales to stockholders' equity
(b) income available to stockholders' equity (return on equity)
(c) operating income to operating assets
(d) sales to net assets
(e) net sales to net working capital.

Another key set of profitability ratios include those that compare different profits or costs to sales. These terms are often expressed in percentage terms. They include:

(a) gross profit to sales
(b) selling expenses to sales
(c) administrative expenses to sales
(d) net profit to sales.

A third way to examine turnover is in relation to CURRENT ASSETS. The key ratios include:

(a) stock to sales

(b) average stock to sales. This ratio is sometimes referred to as the *rate of stock turnover*. It is defined by the formula:

$$\frac{1/2 \text{ (opening stock + closing stock)}}{\text{Sales}}$$

High ratios usually indicate a much larger stockholding than is necessary or that dead stock is being held.

(c) average stock to cost of goods sold.

Trade debtors to sales

Other ratios used to determine profitability and turnover are formulae showing the relationship between sales and trade debtors.

The following formula shows how many times a year a business' debts are paid.

$$\frac{1/2 \text{ (trade debtors + bills receivable at beginning of year + trade debtors + bills receiveable end of year)}}{\text{Sales}}$$

Multiplying this equation by 12 (months), 52 (weeks) or 365 (days) would give an *average collection period* for sales to debts.

Turnover to number of employees

One statistic sometimes sought is turnover earned by the number of employees, i.e. as a percentage of turnover. The employment factor relates to full-time employees. Two part-time employees, that is, persons working between 15 and 30 hours a week, equate to one full-time employee.

The formula for this is:

$$\frac{\text{Turnover}}{1/2 \text{ (number of employees at start of year + number of employees at end of year)}}$$

Example

Model Retailer Limited

1997

$$\frac{\text{Turnover}}{\text{Average number of employees}} = \frac{£480,339}{6} = £80,057$$

Revenue reserves

Revenue reserves arise from a profit made and *retained* at the end of a financial period.

Example

Model Retailer Limited has a retained profit of £4,813 for the year ended 31 May 1997.

This sum is added to reserves held of £10,574 from the year ended 31 May 1996, leaving a retained profit for the year of £15,387.

Profit and Loss Account	1997
	£
Retained profit for the year	4,813
Retained profit brought forward 1 June 1996	10,574
Retained profit carried forward at 31 May 1997	15,387

Dividends may be paid by a company out of profits it has made from either the current or previous years. These accumulated profits, less any dividends that have been paid or declared, will be held in an account such as the PROFIT AND LOSS ACCOUNT and will be described as being *distributable*.

If a profit made does not arise from a bona-fide transaction, such as a revaluation of land and buildings, this profit will be termed a 'non-distributable' profit and will be credited to a separate account such as an *Unrealised profit on revaluation reserve account*.

A sole trade or partnership would not maintain separate reserve accounts but rather credit the year's profit to the owner's or partner's capital or current account. From these accounts, the owner or partner will make his/her drawings on profit.

Salaries, wages and drawings

Salaries

Salaries are sums paid to employees of a company. Although, in a practical sense, they may differ little from wages, they have commonly come to be regarded as sums paid to higher paid employees or staff paid on a monthly basis.

Where salaries or *emoluments* are paid to directors of a company, the information is specified separately.

Wages

Wages, traditionally, are the amounts that are paid weekly to non-managerial staff. Wages commonly reflect those amounts paid to staff who are regarded as a *variable cost* in a company's operating structure.

Drawings

Drawings are the sums taken by the owner of a business, for his personal use, from balances held. Drawings are normally taken from the amount left to a business, after all expenditure, other than tax, has been incurred. Drawings are not a trading item. They are merely an appropriation of profits.

Dividends

Dividends are the method by which owners of a business receive a return on their investment. Where the directors and owners are substantially one and the same, a mix between directors' remuneration and dividends can be arranged to give a favourable tax result.

Shares

Most organisations, particularly those that have more than one owner, define the percentage of the business owned by each party. This percentage is their *share* of that business. The owners of shares in the company are called shareholders.

A company registered under the Companies Act must have a *share capital* comprising shares of fixed value unless it is exempted. Usually these are companies limited by guarantee.

Example

Model Retailer Limited

Notes on Financial Statements 31 May 1997

	Number of shares	£
Equity Share Capital		
Authorised		
Authorised share capital @ £1 each	10,000	10,000
	=====	=====
Allotted called up and fully paid @ £1 each	2	2
	=====	=====

The *authorised share capital* is the maximum number of shares that a company is permitted to issue. This figure is set by its Memorandum of Association. This may be amended at any time by the passing of a resolution by the shareholders.

The total of the *nominal value* of all shares issued by a company comprises its *issued share capital*. In addition to the shares in the issue the company may have further unissued shares. The nominal value can be almost any amount.

The *allotted share capital* is the number of shares that a company has actually issued. This figure can never exceed the authorised share capital. When the shares are initially allotted, their nominal value is referred to as the *called up* capital. As and when they are paid for, they are referred to as *paid up* to the appropriate extent, e.g. '10p Ordinary Shares with 5p paid up'.

If shares are allotted for a value in excess of their nominal value they must be accounted for through a separate account called a *Share Premium Account*. The excess is referred to as the *Share Premium*.

Different classes of shares exist. The nature of the shares will reflect the level of risk entertained by the shareholder. The value of shares held by each party, together with reserves held (see REVENUE RESERVES) are referred to as *shareholders' funds*.

Ordinary shares

Ordinary shares are risk-bearing equity within a company. They are sometimes referred to as *equity shares*. They carry no preferential rights to other shareholders. Through limited liability a shareholder will have his risk limited to the value he has invested in shares in a company. However, where a company's shares are owned by individuals, it is not unusual for a lender to require personal guarantees, in addition to equity offered, as collateral.

Preference shares

Holders of preference shares rank ahead of holders of ordinary shares for dividends and, should the company fail, any distribution. Usually the shares bear fixed interest. Sometimes preference shares are *redeemable*, that is, the shares may be redeemed at a date specified when issued. Funds to pay preference shares are available only from profits.

Stock

Stocks comprise the following categories:

(a) goods or other assets purchased for resale

(b) consumable stores

(c) raw materials and components purchased for incorporation into products for sale

(d) products and services in intermediate stages of completion

(e) long-term contract balances

(f) finished goods.

Stock, merchandise or *inventory* are goods owned by a company that are available for sale to customers.

Within accounts, an organisation's *opening stocks* and *closing stocks* are reflected in the trading account. Opening stocks are the value of the previous year's closing stock.

Example 1

Opening stock (same as last year's closing stock)	£10,000
Plus purchases through the year	£50,000
	£60,000
Less goods sold	£45,000
Closing stock	£15,000
	=======

Example 2

Sometimes opening and closing stocks will be further defined. The accounts of Model Retailer Limited distinguishes between costs of goods purchased from wholesalers and others, and the cost of raw materials used for the manufacture of their own goods.

Cost of sales	£
Opening raw material stock	6,300
Opening stock of finished goods	230,800
Purchases	289,793
Closing raw material stock	(4,200)
Closing stock of finished goods	(231,200)
	291,493

Whether the increase in closing stock is good will depend upon a number of factors that may be identified through RATIO ANALYSIS.

A company's accounts will generally reflect the value of stocks at the lower cost and estimated net selling or disposable value, known as *net realisable value*. Cost is usually computed on a first in, first out basis. Net realisable value is based upon estimated selling price less the estimated cost of their disposal.

Auditors will assess changes in stock quantities between the beginning and end of a financial year, having reviewed records of purchases, production and sales. An audit will also consider appropriate ratios relating to stock and compare it to previous years.

Taxation

The profits from trading are subject to tax. The actual profit shown in the PROFIT AND LOSS ACCOUNT may not be the same figure as is used to calculate the tax due as some expenses are not allowed for tax purposes, for example, entertaining and depreciation. Also, some allowances may be given for tax purposes that do not appear in the profit and loss account, e.g. for certain capital expenditure. These are known as *capital allowances*.

Corporation tax

This will be applied to organisations such as companies. The tax is a liability of the organisation and is payable after a fixed time after the end of the accounting period, normally ten months.

If a company pays a dividend, it must also pay an amount to the Inland Revenue known as *advance corporation tax*. This tax may, subject to certain limits, be offset against the corporation tax due on the profits of the organisation. Where losses are made they may be offset against profits.

Income tax

Where a business is run either as a partnership or by an individual, the profits will be subject to income tax. The tax is a liability of the partners/individual and is payable, normally, in two equal interim instalments on 31 January of the following tax year and 31 July of the tax year after that. If a further final payment is required, this will normally be due on 31 January of that second tax year.

A tax year runs from 6 April in one calendar year to 5 April in the next.

Example

A trader prepares his accounts to 31 December. For the year to 31 December 1996, his taxable profits are £20,000 and the income tax due amounts to £4,000. This tax, arising from profits with a year end in the 1996/97 tax year, will be deemed to be in the 1996/97 tax liability.

£2,000 will be payable on 31 January 1998 and a further £2,000 on 31 July 1998.

There are special rules for when businesses commence or cease, change their year ends or prepare accounts for periods not equal to one year.

Pay as you earn (PAYE)

Pay as you earn is not, strictly speaking, a form of tax but is a method of collecting income tax from an individual's salary. The obligation rests with the employer to deduct the correct amount of tax and to pay this tax to the Inland Revenue on a monthly basis.

If, at the end of a tax year, the Inland Revenue calculate that the individual has either paid too much or not enough it will either make a repayment to the individual or seek to collect the underpayment direct. Sometimes, it will carry the underpayment forward and collect it during the following tax year by notifying the employer to increase the amount of deductions under PAYE.

National Insurance (NI) contributions

National Insurance contributions are payable by partners or an individual on profits from their trading. These will be paid at the same time as the income tax on the profits.

Where a person draws a salary from a company, they will have to pay National Insurance contributions on that salary in addition to the contributions that the company has to pay. These amounts will be payable on a monthly basis along with the PAYE.

Value added tax (VAT)

Value added tax is a tax levied on the value of goods or services provided. Where a business is required to account for VAT, it must register with Her Majesty's Customs and Excise. It will then be required to account to Customs and Excise for the tax that it has charged on its income (outputs) less the tax that has been incurred on expenses or capital expenditure (inputs). If the tax that has been incurred exceeds the tax that has been charged, a repayment can be claimed.

Trial balance

A *trial balance* lists and totals all debit and credit balances taken from an organisation's accounting records at a particular date. If the debits and the credits are not equal, an error has occurred. The error could be:

(a) mathematical (there has been a mistake in calculation)

(b) figure entry (a figure has been incorrectly entered).

As, essentially, a trial balance is a mathematical check, it will not identify items entered incorrectly under the wrong account headings.

In effect, a trial balance will list all balances in a ledger at a given date with the debit balances on one side and the credit balances on the other. Providing the debits and credits are equal in value, the books are said to *balance*. Items missing from different accounts reflected in the trial balance may still result in a mathematical accuracy. Auditor's checking procedures should seek, as far as practicable, to identify any significant errors.

Turnover

Turnover is another term for *sales*. A company's sales are effectively the total of the stock that it sells or turns over in a year.

Example

A company's stock is a constant £1,000,000. It turns its stock over seven times during a year. It therefore has a sales or turnover of £7,000,000.

Sales and turnover are usually expressed in a company's trading account, net of VAT.

Knowledge of a company's predicted turnover is important as it will enable the owners to determine a number of statutory requirements. These include thresholds for VAT and audit.

Turnover value	Legal requirement
Less than £46,000	Deregistration figure for VAT
£48,000 +	Registration for VAT mandatory.
Less than £90,000	Audit may not be necessary for a limited company.
Less than £350,000	A company or organisation can opt for cash accounting method of payment, for VAT purposes.
Between £90,000/£350,000	Full audit may not be necessary but a compilation report will be required.
£195,000 +	Need to complete Intrastat returns for compilation of trade statistics.
£350,000 +	Full audit required.

Value or worth

The *net worth* of a company reflects the total of all assets owed to the owner, less the total of all liabilities.

Cost or *book value* represents the worth of either an individual item or a number of items in a company's accounts. The book value is not the actual sum that can be obtained for an asset. When sold the sum achieved may be greater or lesser than that reflected in a company's books. Book values will generally represent the depreciated value of an ASSET.

Work in progress

Work in progress comprises partially manufactured goods or, in the case of service companies, amounts due but not yet invoiced.

The value attributed to the above, should they be included in accounts, has to be a 'true and fair' reflection of what they are worth. In-depth examinations of these values will need to be undertaken by auditors in fulfilling their duties to the shareholders of a company.

An auditor will wish to determine the *net realisable value* of work in progress. Note will be taken of any aspects which would make that work in progress defective or obsolete. Reasonableness is the key to determining the value. The auditors will look at a value on the basis of a company as a *going concern*.

The value of work in progress will be reflected between accounting periods by:

(a) reconciliation of changes in the value of work in progress at the beginning and end of a financial year

(b) valued judgement on a company's records.

Whilst inclusion of work in progress has the advantage of enhancing a company's asset position, it can also have negative consequences should a company's sales diminish in a following year. Prudence in both the inclusion of work in progress and the value attributed to it should always be exercised.

PART 2
Forms of finance

Asset sale

Assets are property, either intangible or tangible, which have a monetary value.

The assets of a company, providing they have value, may be sold. Indeed, it is not uncommon for large companies to sell parts of their business to another party as a way of generating cash.

Invariably, the sale of an asset has a permanence about it and therefore should not be undertaken without due consideration.

Caution may be necessary when considering the disposal of certain assets, for example, where:

(a) they are used as collateral

(b) their sale may dilute ownership, e.g. sale of shares

(c) the assets may be required at a future date.

It should be noted that assets may have a higher or lower value than their book value (see VALUE OR WORTH).

Often, where expansion is the reason for an asset sale, shares in a company will be disposed of. Alternatively, shares in a company or partnership may be transferred to the vendor, particularly if the sale of shares relates to a merger.

Advantages

The advantages of an asset sale include:

(a) it generates income

(b) unless the asset has a charge over it or is used as collateral, you do not need anyone's permission to sell it.

Disadvantages

The disadvantages of an asset sale include:

(a) the loss of an asset

(b) if the asset sold is shares in a company, or partnership, the vendor may not be able to use proceeds unilaterally.

Example 1

A company is expanding in a new area of business. Certain machinery that was important in its production process has, as a result, become redundant. The machinery is sold generating cash that is then used to buy new, needed equipment.

Example 2

A professional practice wishes to expand. To do so it seeks to purchase a smaller competitor. The smaller competitor agrees to the sale of its business for an appropriate and fair equity holding in the expanded business.

Cash input

Entrepreneurs often need to find money to cover operating costs and especially initial start-up costs. Often the easiest and cheapest method of obtaining finance is to use money held on deposit. Like any other resource, cash available may be limited. The use of liquid assets should not be taken for granted and the loss of flexibility that may result from having less money available should always be carefully assessed.

Advantages

Advantages of a cash input include:

(a) it is readily available
(b) it is a cheap source of finance as no interest is payable
(c) permission is not usually required from others
(d) it does not create a liability to others when used.

Disadvantages

The main disadvantage of a cash input is that it ties up cash that may be needed elsewhere.

Countertrade (barter)

Countertrade is a general term used to describe transactions where goods and services are primarily paid for by the exchange of other goods and services rather than money. Countertrade is often complex. There are, however, many specialists who will assist a company with its countertrade business. Often, it may be possible to assign countertrade obligations to a third party who, for a fee, will absolve the exporter from any further involvement in the countertrade transaction.

Examples of countertrade include:

1. Barter: A direct exchange of goods and services for other goods and services.

2. Counterpurchase: Where goods and services sold are paid for in exchange for other goods or services, less a commission element. The value of the counterpurchase will be less than the value of the export order.

3. Advance purchase: This is similar to counterpurchase except that the vendor releases his goods or services first.

4. Buyback: Where the vendor agrees to full or part payment in the form of goods in an enterprise which has an interest.

5. Tolling: In this situation the supplier is treated as an outdoor contractor and the purchaser finances the purchase of all raw materials. The customer will retain ownership of the raw material.

6. Offset: Under offset the supplier agrees to use goods and services provided by the importer.

Advantages

Advantages of countertrade include:

(a) cash may not be required

(b) it allows for trade with organisations (often countries) with no cash.

Disadvantages:

The disadvantages of countertrade include:

(a) it is often difficult to construct an agreement
(b) control of the agreement may be difficult
(c) it cannot be hidden from normal trading procedures
(d) it may lead to a tax liability.

Example

Company A, a consultancy practice, suffers a loss for which it calls in an insurance assessor to negotiate a claim. The assessor, requiring company A's services, agrees to waive her fee providing company A does likewise.

Both companies, by this simple barter arrangement, have benefited without money changing hands.

Where a barter agreement results in either the acquisition or disposal of assets, the transaction will need to be recorded in a company's accounts. Where a profit is made, the company may have to pay tax on this.

A useful publication entitled *Countertrade and Offset – A Guide for Exporters* is available through the Overseas Trade Services. Contact: DTI Export Publications, ADMAIL 528, London SW1W 8YT. Tel: 0171 510 0171, Fax: 0171 510 0197.

Credit and charge cards

Company or personal credit cards may be used to obtain finance for a business. The granting of a credit card is predetermined and, as with an overdraft facility, does not need to be used. Typically, credit cards would be used for short-term finance to purchase an asset of £10,000 or less or to pay for a business expense, for example, an overseas business trip. Credit cards should be used as convenience cards rather than as a key form of business finance.

Credit cards differ from charge cards in that they can offer an extended credit period, albeit at higher rates of interest whilst charge cards must be settled in full by the due date.

Advantages

Advantages of credit and charge cards include:

(a) once permission has been granted, total flexibility to spend money up to a credit limit, on whatever goods or services one chooses

(b) they are internationally acceptable; overseas expenses can be paid in the currency required

(c) the goods and services purchased are covered by insurance

(d) there can be more than one cardholder, thereby negating the need for special permissions and requests for money

(e) they provide a very cheap form of instant credit, providing sums are paid off immediately.

Disadvantages

Disadvantages of credit and charge cards include:

(a) they are an expensive form of borrowing if not settled immediately, particularly if cash is withdrawn

(b) scrutiny has to be observed if there is more than one cardholder; cardholders can have individual credit limits

(c) they may be insecure if cards are not kept carefully.

Customer credit facilities

Credit facilities offered by suppliers are perhaps the most common form of finance available to businesses. The length of credit offered can vary considerably, depending on the agreement negotiated. The allowing or granting of credit is a declaration of confidence that an agreement for the sale or purchase of goods and services will be honoured. Where payment is made earlier than a due date, a supplier will often provide a discount. Equally, where payments are late, interest may be charged.

The supply of goods and services on credit is flexible and allows trade between organisations without the necessity of a credit check on each occasion. The supplier of goods and services is always recommended to check the financial viability of his customer or client and to monitor the level of business and payments made.

Advantages

Offering customer credit facilities:

(a) is flexible

(b) is easy to administer

(c) allows business to be conducted immediately, on the basis of a later payment.

Disadvantages

Disadvantages of offering customer credit facilities include:

(a) payment is not instant

(b) it may be difficult to collect payment once goods have been released or services supplied

(c) legal procedures may not always negate a loss.

(d) dependence on credit facilities, rather than profits, can lead to cash flow problems.

Example

A purchaser wishes to buy 1,000 pairs of slippers at £1.50 each. The vendor takes a credit reference out on the purchaser and discovers that the sale of goods up to a value of £5,000 would be acceptable. Once terms of trade have been agreed and a firm order placed, goods are released on a payment basis of 30 days, nett.

Export finance

Exporters, unlike vendors on the home market, have to consider many risks inherent in dealing with a customer in a foreign country where collection of a debt may not be easy or possible. In addition to trading risks involving the individual customer, there may be country risks, for example, due to political or economic instability.

To enable such trade to happen, both banks and a number of specialist organisations provide facilities to exporters, usually backed by insurance, to cover such contingencies. Costs of this provision would depend upon the nature of the customer and country with whom trade is being conducted.

Whilst a CREDIT FACILITY – called *open account* – or cash transaction may allow for the easy sale of goods and services overseas, the following methods of finance and insurance are common.

Letters of credit

A letter of credit is a means by which importers and exporters agree to buy and sell goods through the intermediary of a bank. Through this procedure the exporter, in effect, sells its goods to one bank and the buyer accepts the risk of receiving faulty or late goods with another bank.

Both parties benefit. The exporter will benefit owing to the certainty of payment. The importer benefits owing to the certainty of terms and conditions being fulfilled.

Most letters of credit are irrevocable. If they are well constructed, they can allow for the importer's bank to pay an agreed sum even if there are minor discrepancies.

The importer, being the party to pay for the goods, would advise his bank of documents he wishes to see before money is released to the exporter. Such documents would usually include bills of lading (proof that the goods are with a carrier), invoices, packing notes, quality control certificates and insurance certificates if goods are sold cost, insurance, freight (CIF) included. These documents would be sent by the importer's bank, which is called the *opening* or *issuing bank*, to an international bank or *advising bank*. The advising bank will then pass documents to the exporter. The exporter will present the documentation to his bank. Should the exporter not agree to certain of the conditions stipulated, he would need to get the importer to change those terms. On the assumption that the terms stipulated are acceptable, the exporter would manufacture and/or despatch goods in accordance with the contractual obligations stated within the letter of credit. Equally, money would be released by the importer's bank, in accordance with those agreed conditions.

Bills of exchange

A bill of exchange is an unconditional promise to pay a fixed amount at a fixed date. The bill will be addressed to the exporter or *drawee* and signed by the importer or *drawer*. As bills are often used to regulate the possession of goods, they are often accompanied by title documents.

Credit insurance

To mitigate the risk that may be associated with export, suppliers may obtain many different forms of credit insurance to protect them against customer or country risks. Short-term credit insurance can readily be obtained from commercial banks, a number of private sector companies or brokers.

Payment guarantees

Payment guarantees are a form of export insurance that allow exporters to receive payment once goods are physically exported. Two types are relevant for smaller businesses. These include:

1. Supply and credit: This allows payment for the goods exported on a single transaction.

2. Lines of credit: These enable money to be issued against contracts on a continuing or rolling basis. The minimum value of such contracts would usually be in the region of $25,000, (£14,700).

These forms of insurance are available from major high street banks and the Exports Credits Guarantee Department (ECGD).

Finance facilities

The financing of long-term projects, especially for contracts for supply of capital or project goods or services, may require the help of specialists such as the Export Credits Guarantee Department (ECGD). Through the ECGD, banks will issue finance to companies on accepted contracts, where payment is made by a promissory note or a bill of exchange, on the basis that the ECGD provides a guarantee against default. Such provision may be for either a single transaction or a number of different contracts with the same customer. Such facilities are aimed specifically at contracts lasting two years or more. It is also a requirement that 15% of the contract value should be paid by the buyer before the credit period commences.

Contact ECGD, PO Box 2200, 2 Exchange Tower, Harbour Exchange Square, London E14 9GS. Tel: 0171-512 7887. Fax: 0171-512 7268, or view the Web site at http://www.open.gov.uk/ecgd/.

Export factoring

Factoring for export trade has grown considerably over the past decade. It is available to companies with an export turnover of £75,000 or more. Factoring is referred to in greater detail on page 102.

Advantages

The advantages of export factoring include:

(a) access to money tied up in export debtors

(b) knowledge of export market including its language, trading terms to be used, customs and legal methods of redress

(c) advice on credit risks can be included

(d) negates the need for the exporter to do research

(e) bad debt protection insurance can be included

(f) protection against exchange risk when invoicing in a foreign currency may be provided.

(g) stated countries or customers may be covered, if agreed in advance

(h) knowledge of a potential customer may be persuasive in encouraging you to undertake that trade without security

(i) the factor will be responsible for payment of debts in sterling.

Disadvantages

The disadvantage of export factoring is that it can be costly for certain countries.

Factoring and invoice discounting

Factoring and discounting companies provide three main services that can be taken in any combination, either within the UK or internationally. These are:

1. Finance: Secured against the outstanding invoices of the business.

2. Credit management: The outsourcing of the sales ledger and credit control system to a factoring company.

3. Credit protection: To protect clients against bad debts.

Depending on the combination of these, the service is known as either factoring or invoice discounting.

Factoring and invoice discounting are financial facilities designed to improve the cashflow of a business by converting debts on unpaid invoices into cash. By factoring or invoice discounting, a business will sell its invoices to the factor or discounter once they are issued. In return, they will receive up to 80% of the invoice value in cash, normally within 24 hours of the invoice being transferred. The balance, less any agreed charges, will be paid to the business after a set period, or when the debt has been collected. Factoring is generally associated with fast-growing companies or those where working capital is increasingly tied up in unpaid invoices.

Factoring

Factoring involves a business contracting out its sales ledger and debt collection to a factor. The factoring may be *non-recourse factoring* by which the factor will purchase all approved book debts and the risk associated with them should there be a default. By *recourse factoring*, the factor will be able to seek payment from a customer for any bad debt that it incurs.

Advantages

The main advantages of factoring are that:

(a) it provides finance against invoices, thereby meeting any increase in turnover.

(b) the factor pays their customer upon receipt of issued invoices

(c) it provides instant access to money that would otherwise be tied up in debtors

(d) payments from factors are predictable, i.e. you know when money will arrive

(e) it sustains cashflow

(f) the credit control function is passed to the factor

(g) the factor pursues late payers

(h) it can include bad debt protection insurance

(i) the factor will advise customer on creditworthiness of potential customers

(j) not all customers need to be included, but agreement must be obtained on this at the outset

(k) it does not require security on assets outside of the debtors list

(l) it is contractual and therefore cannot be withdrawn at whim

(m) the client can choose to trade at a higher level or with customers not accepted, though, bad debt protection will only apply to the credit limit with agreed customers

(n) a factor is often perceived as a legal entity and therefore is paid faster by debtors.

Disadvantages

The main disadvantages of factoring are that:

(a) it is usually only available to companies with turnovers in excess of £50,000

(b) a spread of customer is usually required, with no single debtor being responsible for more than 40% of the total outstanding debt

(c) it is not generally available to companies dealing directly with private individuals or the general public

(d) it is not generally available to professions or organisations whose income is fee-based

(e) it will not cover extended invoice payments, for example, monthly standing orders payable over a period of a year

(f) it relinquishes control of debts and their payment to a third party

(g) if a factor falls into receivership its customers would be regarded as ordinary creditors. However, apart from one instance in the early 1990s, this has not occurred.

Invoice discounting

Through *invoice discounting*, the onus and responsibility for collecting debts remains with the customer. The finance company simply provides money against expected receipts and little else.

Advantages

The advantages of invoice discounting include:

(a) retaining control of sales ledger
(b) invoices are sent out under company's own name
(c) the company does not relinquish control of debts
(d) it is similar in cost to a bank overdraft rate
(e) payments are sent to the customer.

Disadvantages

The disadvantages are that it is not available to businesses with turnovers of less than £750,000, and that it is subject to most of the disadvantages associated with factoring (see above).

Cost

The cost of factoring ranges from approximately 0.5% to 3% over bank base rate. The cost of invoice discounting, where finance alone is selected, ranges between 0.2% and 0.5% of turnover. The factor or discounter will also charge a service fee of between 1% and 2.5%.

For further information contact: Factors and Discounters Association, 18 Upper Grosvenor Street, London W1X 9PB. Tel: 0171 290 6938; Fax: 0171 290 6924.

Most high street banks have factors and invoice discounters associated with them.

Merchant finance

One relatively new scheme for obtaining finance for a business is through merchant finance. Through this method, goods are technically sold to a merchant financier, who is invoiced directly. The merchant financier then invoices your customer, with the manufacturer acting as their sales agent. Once confirmation of the acceptance of goods has been received, the merchant financier will release up to 80% of the sales invoice value to you, with the balance less commission being released when they are paid.

Advantages

Advantages include:

(a) merchant financiers provide additional finance to your normal requirements

(b) unlike factoring, individual customers or invoices may be financed.

Disadvantages

Disadvantages include:

(a) many banks perceive a merchant financier as a factor not a debtor

(b) a bank may offset any merchant finance agreement by lowering other credit arrangements

(c) it is more costly than factoring.

Gifts in kind

Gifts in kind or *donations,* are often relevant for charities or organisations that are favoured by individuals or organisations, for example, schools. Whilst account should be taken of gifts in kind in an organisation's accounts, it is often impractical.

Gifts in kind may take many forms but commonly include:

(a) free use of premises
(b) free use of equipment
(c) loan of staff.

Example

A registered charity wishes to arrange a conference. A hotel agrees to waive its charge for a conference room. As a result, money that would have been needed for such a facility is no longer necessary.

Applications by registered charities for financial support should always list gifts in kind. A project that may cost £20,000, for which £10,000 of facilities and staffing are provided at no cost, could be said to have found half the money required. This is often important when grants are only given to organisations that are able to secure a large part of project funding themselves.

Grants

A source of finance often overlooked by businesses is government and other grants. A number of factors may determine eligibility for this support. These may include the creation of new jobs, the purchase of plant and machinery or the refurbishment of a building. Grant availability is often location-dependent. Where grants are offered, their purpose is to encourage and persuade an organisation to proceed with a project it would not otherwise undertake or carry out in the same way. Thus, if you have already started a project or if it is nearing completion, you are unlikely to receive a grant.

Should a grant be offered it would be to assist a company with its project, not to fully fund it or bail it out of a problem. It is unusual for grants to exceed 25% of eligible capital expenditure or, in the case of grants towards consultancy and training projects, 50% of the external costs involved. In view of this, an applicant must consider other sources of funding.

Finding out about grants, in itself, is not complex. Free information for investment projects is readily available from appropriate government departments such as the DTI (local office or 0171 215 5000) and many local authorities. The Training Enterprise Councils (TECs) in England and Wales and (LECs) Local Enterprise Councils in Scotland hold details on employment and training grants. A range of support is available to exporters. The DTI, through the Overseas Trade Services, publishes a free guide to export services entitled *Exporting* (Ref: URN 95/898 – January 1996). This may be obtained by telephoning 0171 510 0174. The Offices of the European Commission (Tel: 0171 973 1992) produces two useful publications: *Europe: Funding from the Fourth Framework Programme for Research and Technological Development* (1994 to 1998) and *Finance from Europe*.

Some high street banks offer free searches on grants to existing and prospective customers. The information provided is variable. Grant searches are also offered by Business Link (Tel: 0345 567765). Business Link is a country-wide organisation offering free, independent business advice. Although many Business Link offices do offer an excellent service, others have been harshly criticised. They may also charge a fee of around £20 for a grant search.

You should be cautious about using firms that claim that all you need do to be entitled to many tens or even hundreds of thousands of pounds is to part with a fee of about £300. Firms offering these services are often the subject of critical television programmes and newspaper reports.

You should always take reasonable precautions to check the pedigree and reliability of any firm offering grant services. There are many excellent firms, ranging from highly specialist companies, concentrating on one or two types of grants to general practitioners. Often such organisations will work on a no result, no fee basis. The most important thing to remember is not to determine 'what is available' but 'what is available and of use'.

When applying for grants, you will usually be required to submit a proposal or business plan to the grantor. The complexity of such applications does vary. Generally, a grantor will assist you in completing application forms. A grantor will, however, expect you to have thought about your project and expect you to be able to provide relevant information.

Whilst manufacturing companies tend to be favourably considered for grant applications, this should not discourage service industries or even those in professions. Outside employment and training issues, many other grants have been awarded to such organisations. These have been most successfully obtained in cases where the service company is a specialist trading nationally or supplies a niche market.

Grants for manufacturing and specialist service industries

Manufacturers may wish to look at grants such as Regional Selective Assistance. This grant, which is negotiable, aims at helping most companies in Assisted Areas with projects in which there is both capital expenditure and job creation.

Grants for research and development

The DTI also has a number of schemes suitable for inventors including the SMART award and SPUR. Details of these two schemes can be obtained from your nearest government office.

Grants for property development

Grants for property development may be available. Contact English Partnerships (Tel: 0171 976 7070) for their investment guide. For firms in rural areas a wide range of support may be available through the Rural Development Commission (Tel: 01722 336255). Should your building be listed, advice should be sought from the Historic Buildings and Monuments Commission for England (English Heritage) or its equivalent in Scotland, Wales or Northern Ireland.

You should also remember that each case is considered on its own merits. Grantors like nothing better than to help a company to succeed. However, success is dependent upon them having the confidence in your project. Should your proposal be acceptable, it is likely that you will receive some support.

Grants for employment and training

A range of support exists to help with the recruitment of staff towards their initial and ongoing development and training. Many TECs and LECs provide support for schemes, usually administered through agents, to partly fund these costs. Some prefer the short, sharp approach using work trials to get people into work. Others prefer a longer term solution using customised training as their method of delivery. Many local authorities, often with the backing of European Union money from the European Social Fund, also provide incentives to create jobs in their areas. Both directly and indirectly, many capital-related grants such as Regional Selective Assistance are based upon the twin pillars of capital expenditure and job creation.

Financial assistance to develop firms, is also available through the TECs through 'Skills for Small Businesses' and 'Investors in People'. These schemes encourage firms to review where they are in terms of their performance, devise an action plan to improve upon this, implement changes recommended and then evaluate their position again for further development.

Soft loan support of up to £5,000 per employee, to a maximum of £250,000, may be available through high street banks to cover approved training costs under the Small Firms Loan Guarantee Scheme.

Grants for consultancy

For many years, British governments have held the view that external advice can provide a valuable insight into the operation of a business and give owners the ability to control business outcomes. The key mechanism for providing consultancy to clients is through Business Link (Tel 0345 567765), TECs (Freefone 0800 834247) and, in Scotland, LECs). The work of the TECs and LECs has been referred to above. Business Link provides consultancy support to local businesses of all sizes wishing to develop and grow as well as to those wishing to move to the area each office covers. Business Connect in Wales, and the Local Enterprise Development Agency (LEDU) and the Industrial Development Board (IDB), both of which are in Northern Ireland, and Scottish Business Shops provide similar advice.

Two related programmes, the Diagnostic Service (advice) and Consultancy Service (implementation) may provide some financial assistance towards consultancy projects. Many other bodies will also provide support towards consultancy, including the Rural Development Commission and some local authorities.

Grants for exporters

A wide range of organisations will provide advice and support, often subsidised, to potential and existing exporters. The DTI is the main source of such provision, whether it be directly through subsidised schemes, or indirectly through grants administered by the British Chambers of Commerce or trade associations. Some TECs, LECs and local authorities also provide minor assistance to help exporters. In many areas, Business Link offers hands-on advice through export development counsellors.

Substantial incentives may be available to companies wishing to establish a presence overseas, particularly if it involves a joint venture operation with a foreign company. The Foreign and Commonwealth Office and the European Union both offer financial assistance for projects of this nature.

Grants from the European Union (EU)

Although each member state of the EU provides its own programmes for support to sectors of the economy, the European Commission tries to foster a common approach, looking at the European Union as a political, social and economic entity. Supported programmes, covering almost every aspect of life within the Community, are regulated by Directorate Generales. Through Structural Funds, substantial funding is given to organisations undertaking programmes that will correct or benefit those regions in which severe social and economic problems prevail. This funding is generally administered through appropriate government departments, local authorities and governmental and business agencies. Some help, for example, European Coal and Steel Closure Area loans and European Investment Bank loans, may be administered through banks.

Whilst loan schemes and structural funding may be the more usual form of support given to SMEs (Small and Medium Size Enterprises), the financial assistance most regularly referred to is that for research and development. Support offered through the EU aims to maintain and enhance the Community's economic and technological position in the face of competition from the USA and Japan. Other funding, with the same aim, is that given to countries in the Third World and, most significantly, in Central and Eastern Europe and the new independent states of the former Soviet Union.

Grants for agriculture, horticulture and aquaculture

Many schemes are available to help both farmers and manufacturers of food products. Manufacturers will often be able to obtain support from traditional sources such as the DTI, subject to their eligibility. Producers of prime goods, through a variety of mechanisms, enacted by the European Union and regulated by the Ministry of Agriculture, Fisheries and Food are able to obtain support for these. Where there is over-capacity in the market, subsidies may be provided to discourage production that would not be able to be sold without causing severe dislocation to the market-place.

Grants from other sources

Whilst a number of sources of support have been referred to, you would be prudent to keep an open mind on other areas from which financial assistance may be obtained. Many sources of advice, help and financial assistance are available. Access to these depends on making a sensible and considered approach. The companies that have proven to be the most successful in obtaining help are those that do not approach sources of funding with tunnel vision, but are open and susceptible to new approaches and ideas. Equally, these companies have not sought help without first reviewing their own standing in the market-place and considering the products, services and methods to be used to take their organisation forward.

Advantages and disadvantages relating to grant offers

Advantages

The advantage of using grants include:

(a) many grants are easily obtainable

(b) grants are non-repayable if conditions are fulfilled

(c) grant monies may be staged according to need

(d) some grants may be paid in full, or part, in advance. This, however, is rare.

Disadvantages

The disadvantages of using grants include:

(a) many grants take time to negotiate

(b) doing project work before a grant is approved may make you ineligible

(c) grant payments are usually triggered after expenditure on a project, or job creation, has taken place

(d) monitoring may be strict and inflexible, though problems of this nature may be avoided providing professional advice is taken and that the grant-awarding body is kept informed

(e) grants may take longer to negotiate than anticipated.

Hire purchase

Hire purchase (HP) is a medium-term source of finance appropriate for the purchase of capital equipment including vehicles. HP terms will vary according to:

(a) the amount borrowed
(b) the period of agreement
(c) the regularity of payment.

Hire purchase agreements are usually brokered through finance houses. These are associated with or owned by high street banking groups. Being specialists, they are often able to give a competitive and quick response to a request for financial support.

Advantages

Advantages of using hire purchase include:

(a) most suppliers of capital equipment offer HP, or alternatively it is regularly available through banks and other lending sources

(b) for tax purposes, equipment purchased under HP may attract capital allowances

(c) assets purchased revert to the borrower at the end of the period

(d) there is no VAT on monthly or other payments

(e) the length of the agreement is known

(f) payment terms are fixed throughout the term of the agreement, which assists budgeting and cashflow decisions

(g) goods purchased on HP are regarded as an asset of the company for grant claims, the contractual obligation to complete the purchase being paramount.

Disadvantages

Disadvantages of using hire purchase include:

(a) there is usually a need to place a deposit and one or more months payments in advance

(b) goods purchased under HP cannot be used as security as title remains with the lender until the agreement ends

(c) it can be expensive to withdraw from an HP agreement.

Example

A business owner wishes to purchase a vehicle. The negotiated cost of the car comes to £14,000, a sum the owner is unable to afford in the short-term period. After payment of a deposit of £4,000, HP for the balance, payable over a four-year term, at £280 per month including insurance protection, is agreed.

As a result of HP, the purchaser is able to drive away with the car and the vendor receives money from a finance company for the vehicle sold.

The title of the vehicle falls to the finance company whilst ownership and use is available to the borrower.

Joint venture

A joint venture is an operation where two or more organisations and/or individuals 'join' together for an ongoing business proposition. The basis of joint ventures is that each party will have something to add to the venture, be it money, expertise, contacts, or industrial or service base upon which to expand. The proportion of the business or partnership owned will be matter of negotiation.

Example

A manufacturer of wooden toys wishes to develop a new product. A business associate wishes to offer financial backing, but only in respect of the new product range. An agreement for a joint venture reflecting the expertise of the manufacturer and the financial input of the joint venture investing partner is drawn up and signed.

Advantages

Advantages of a joint venture include:

(a) it enables business partners with different assets and attributes to work on a project

(b) it is a short-term means of raising finance

(c) finance is focused on a particular aspect of a business

(d) the risk is shared.

Disadvantages

Disadvantages of a joint venture include:

(a) any commercial success would be shared

(b) the proposer may not have full control over decision-making in the joint venture

(c) there may be an increase in administrative burden, for example, separate records may need to be kept

(d) administration may be problematic unless roles and rewards are clearly assigned.

Leasing

The statement of Standard Accounting Practice No. 21 defines as lease as 'a contract between a lessor and a lessee for the hire of specific assets. The lessor retains ownership of the asset but gives right to the use of the asset to the lessee for an agreed period of time in return for the payment of specified rentals.'

Leasing is available for buildings, machinery and vehicles, and enables an organisation to use an asset for a fixed period of time. At the end of that period the asset reverts to the owner. Some leasing arrangements, for example, *finance leasing*, enable the lessee to acquire the asset for a nominal sum at the end of the lease period. Leasing agreements lasting less than one year are often referred to as rental agreements or licences.

Another common form of operating lease is *contract hire*. Through contract hire the lessor undertakes responsibility for management and maintenance of the capital equipment, usually vehicles.

Advantages

The advantages of leasing include:

(a) the borrower or lessee can determine how long he wants the asset for

(b) leasing arrangements for property may include a rent-free period.

(c) payment periods are pre-determined, though rent reviews may be required for property transactions

(d) a business can generally deduct the cost of rent from taxable income, as a trading expense

(e) long-term leases (ten years or more) may be capitalised for some grant purposes.

Disadvantages

The disadvantages of leasing include:

(a) can be expensive if early termination is requested

(b) assets cannot be used as collateral, as ownership never passes to the lessee

(c)   pre-payments of the rental sum are usually required
(d)   deposits are sometimes required
(e)   the lessee may need to insure and maintain the asset
(f)   the leasing company claims capital allowances.

Example 1

A garment manufacturer obtains a substantial order for clothing requiring a special type of machine. The order is unlikely to be repeated and purchase of the machinery would be prohibitive. Contract hire is arranged for the period of six months, this being the time required to manufacture these particular goods.

Example 2

A business expands and needs new premises. It is not known how long the business will require the premises for, but the duration is estimated to be at least five years before any further expansion is undertaken. Suitable premises are found on which a ten-year lease is negotiated, with a break clause after five years.

Loans for capital expenditure

Methods of borrowing money to finance a project often vary according to the reason for the request. Some forms of borrowing have become associated with particular items, for example, hire purchase for plant, machinery and vehicles, and mortgages for buildings. The usual source for this finance would be a bank. Bank loans will be examined in greater detail in LOANS FOR WORKING CAPITAL.

Although the distinction between different types of loans may be blurred, this section will look at loans requested for substantial, general asset-backed projects. The following section will examine sources of finance used for financing operational expenditure.

British Coal Enterprise

British Coal Enterprise loans are dependent upon job creation and capital expenditure. The amount of loan is calculated on the basis of £5,000 per new job created or 25% of the total financial requirement, whichever sum is the smaller.

Contact the following regional offices for more details:

Midlands Region – 01623 442244
Northern Region – 0191 4913888
Scotland Region – 01259 218021
South Wales Region – 01222 813001
Western Region – 01925 234924
Yorkshire Region – 01302 727228

British Steel (Industry) Limited

BS(I) offers loans and share capital ranging from £10,000 to £150,000 to businesses based within the 20 traditional steel industry areas. Interest rates are set close to base rates and are fixed for the period of the loan. Usually these run for two to four years. Loans of up to £25,000 may be made on an unsecured basis. BS(I) loans and share capital packages are generally available to manufacturing businesses and industrial service businesses.

Contact the following regional offices for more details:

North of England – 01642 244633
Yorkshire and Humberside – 0114 2700933
Wales – 01222 471122
Scotland – 01698 845045

European Coal and Steel Community (ECSC) loans

The ECSC, through its subsidised loan scheme, seeks to encourage investment in areas affected by the decline and closure of coal mines or steel works, thereby stimulating job creation.

Loans are available for up to 50% of eligible capital expenditure with a single bullet repayment for the capital sum being demanded five years after the money is drawn. A bank, personal or asset-backed guarantee, amounting to 120% of the value of the loan will be sought. The loans, which have varied in recent years between 2% to 3% above base rate, are fixed. However, the greatest advantage to these loans is that a 3% interest rebate is paid following evidence of job creation, with each job being valued at £11,000 for rebate purposes. Loans of less than £7.5 million are handled nationally through high street banks or development agencies. Experience has shown that only banks or development agencies in coal and steel closure areas tend to be familiar with this scheme.

A number of sectors, mostly outside manufacturing, are ineligible for ECSC loan support.

Example

The Acme Company wants to buy a new factory and equipment costing £1 million. In addition to capital purchases, 25 new jobs are to be created. A loan application for £500,000, at a fixed interest rate of 7.9% is made available for the project by a high street bank administering the loan. In addition, a 3% rebate for jobs created, resulting in a net interest rate of 4.9% is awarded for the period of five years on the sum of £275,000. This latter sum equates to 25 jobs at £11,000 each.

European Investment Bank (EIB) –- EIB–funded schemes

Term debt for SMEs (Small and Medium Size Enterprises) may be available from UK banks and leasing companies under EIB-funded schemes. Under these schemes, the individual loans may be from about £50,000 up to about

£10 million, and may be obtained for a variety of projects in manufacturing or service industries. Unlike ECSC loans (see above), there are no job creation criteria.

For further details contact:

Barclays Bank Plc – 0171 382 8032
Barclays Mercantile Business Finance Limited – 01256 791690/791599
Forward Trust Business Finance Limited – 0121 455 4594
Lloyds Bowmaker Limited – 01202 552077
Lombard Business Finance – 01737 734111
Midland Bank Plc – 0114 252 9316
NWS Bank Plc – 01244 693340
RoyScot Trust Plc – 01242 634183

Local Authority loans

A number of local authorities will provide loans to new and growing businesses. Funding offered tends to be start-up finance for new businesses. It may also be available where there is a good project and where the business is likely to produce employment or other benefits to the local area. Eligibility rules are strictly adhered to and applicants are advised to make enquiries from their local authority. Loans offered tend to be at, or even slightly above, market rate. Local authorities will often only assist as lenders of last resort.

Many local authority loans are handled indirectly by local financial organisations, enterprise agencies or Business Link.

Loans for working capital

Obtaining support for working capital may be more difficult for a business to acquire than that for a physical asset. Such borrowing often becomes blurred as the finance may be needed for both assets and general operations. A principle often stated is 'not to borrow short for items required over a long period'. One of the methods of borrowing short is by use of overdraft finance. Long-term loans, often taken out on the basis of an existing asset, for example, by mortgaging or re-mortgaging a property, are referred to in the previous and following sections. Loans for working capital will almost inevitably be based upon collateral available. The security most likely to be requested is a charge against a single asset, such as a house. For large loans, a DEBENTURE may be sought.

Bank loans (high street banks)

Bank loans, which are often used for asset purchase, may also be used to finance the running of a business. A bank loan will outline the amounts borrowed, the terms of repayment and the amount of interest to be paid, and the method by which this is determined. Some loans allow for early repayment. Security will usually be required by the lender. The nature of the security, whether based upon assets, stock or invoices, will vary according to many factors including the relationship of the borrower to the lender and the confidence that the latter has in the business propositions put forward.

Occasionally, where overdraft facilities tend to be constantly used, a lender may suggest that part of hard core debt is converted into a loan. The advantages and disadvantages of doing this have to be carefully considered.

Advantages

Advantages of converting an overdraft into a loan includes:

(a) the amount borrowed is determined from the outset

(b) terms are established on negotiation

(c) terms may include insurance against default

(d) only one arrangement fee will be charged

(e) the terms may include a capital repayment holiday.

Disadvantages

The disadvantages of a loan conversion include:

(a) there will be an administration and negotiation fee, although this can be included in the loan amount

(b) security is likely to be required

(c) penalty clauses may be included for early repayment

(d) terms may be non-negotiable

(e) insurance may be required to be taken alongside the loan.

Loans (other sources)

Many sources of loans other than high street banks exist. Take care, when obtaining such loans, to ensure that the lender is reputable. Often, these lenders will provide finance as lenders of last resort. As lenders of high-risk loans, interest rates are likely to be high. Sometimes, these are local authorities. Equally, some lenders may be personally connected to the borrower.

Advantages

Advantages of borrowing from non-standard sources include:

(a) loan may be inexpensive if from a close connection
(b) terms and conditions known from the outset
(c) terms may sometimes be re-negotiated.

Disadvantages

Disadvantage of borrowing from non-standard sources includes:

(a) loan may be expensive

(b) loan may be subject to stringent penalties should a problem with repayments occur

(c) loan may be subject to disadvantages similar to those of high street bank loans

(d) terms may be non-negotiable.

The Small Firms Loan Guarantee Scheme (LGS)

The Small Firms Loan Guarantee Scheme (LGS) may be available to help viable firms that are unable to obtain a conventional loan, owing to a lack of collateral available, to obtain additional finance required for their business.

Under this scheme the government provides lenders, who are mostly high street banks, with a guarantee against default by new and existing businesses on loans offered up to the sum of £250,000. Sums greater than £100,000 are available only to organisations that have been operating for two or more years. Terms of the loan are usually between two and ten years.

In addition to the advantages and disadvantages usual for high street bank loans (see page 122), the following should also be considered.

Advantages

Advantages of the LGS include:

(a) aimed to assist businesses with a poor asset base
(b) it may include capital holiday repayments of up to two years.

Disadvantages

Disadvantages of the LGS include:

(a) a premium payment of 1.5% of the loan for variable rate lending or 0.5% of the loan for fixed rate lending will be required

(b) loans will not be guaranteed for businesses in the finance, property or many service sectors

(c) stringent requirements for regular information may be imposed.

Merchant banks

Where sums in excess of £250,000 are required, propositions could be put to merchant banks. Generally, these do not provide finance for periods of more than five years but do access other sources where and when appropriate.

Mortgages

Mortgages are a form of long-term finance taken to:

(a) acquire land or existing buildings
(b) refinance a currently owned property
(c) expand existing properties.

The amount offered is generally in the region of 70% of the freehold value of land and buildings and 60% for a long leasehold, that is, where the lease exceeds 40 years. Mortgage finance is cheaper than other forms of bank borrowing as it is both asset-backed and long term. However, initial costs involved in setting up a mortgage can be expensive owing to surveying, bank and legal fees. Mortgages are widely available through many sources including banks, building societies and insurance companies and some financial institutions. Although many business people may take out or increase the mortgage on their home to obtain funding for a business project, the forms of mortgage described below will be those generally relating to commercial property.

You are advised to obtain independent financial advice as to the suitability of any mortgage arrangement to be undertaken.

Forms of commercial mortgage

There are a number of commercial mortgages available:

(a) *Repayment mortgage*: Repayment mortgages provide for the repayment of both interest and the capital sum over a fixed period of time. Initially, most of the repayments will be for interest, which is calculated in advance. From the middle towards the end period of a mortgage, the payments will account mostly for the capital sum. Changes in interest rates may affect the interest charged. At the end of the mortgage period, the borrower will have no liability to the lender.

(b) *Convertible mortgage*: Convertible mortgages allow lenders to share long-term capital appreciation in the property required. Generally, the lender will place a fixed charge over the property and the borrower will grant an option to purchase the property at a later date. Should the option not be taken up, the borrower will pay the lender an agreed minimum sum.

(c) *Participating mortgage*:   In these mortgages, the lender will receive an agreed percentage of the value of property at the end of the loan period.

Advantages

Advantages of commercial mortgages include:

(a) they are readily available, providing property is good security

(b) they are a cheaper form of finance

(c) terms may be re-negotiated if property requirements or nature of property changes, e.g. increases in value owing to a building extension

(d) terms may allow for capital repayment holiday.

Disadvantages

Disadvantages of commercial mortgages include:

(a) there may be penalty clauses for early repayment

(b) the borrower may be required to take out insurance should there be a default in payment terms

(c) the lender may require keyman insurance i.e. insurance to be taken out on principal staff

(d) foreclosure proceedings may be undertaken by the lender if repayments not met.

Overdraft

An overdraft facility is the most common form of short-term borrowed finance used by businesses in the United Kingdom. They are often preferred by businesses as they are a flexible method of obtaining finance needed and, unlike loans, do not have a permanence in terms of years.

The cost or arrangement fee for setting up an overdraft facility ranges between 0.5% and 3% with interest rates charged on overdrafts used being up to 7% above base rate.

Overdrafts, like other forms of bank finance, will usually require that the borrower has security to cover the amount offered.

Overdrafts should be avoided for long-term debt situations as they are an expensive form of borrowing. In practice, the overdraft is used as a form of core funding for many businesses. Recognising this, many banks now prefer their small business customers (with turnovers of less than £100,000) to take out a business loan.

Advantages

Advantages of an overdraft include:

(a) these are a flexible form of borrowing to a fixed limit
(b) the customer pays interest only on the amount used
(c) working within overdraft facilities is flexible
(d) overdraft interest payments are tax-deductible.

Disadvantages

Disadvantages of overdrafts include:

(a) they are expensive, particularly if agreed limits are exceeded
(b) they are subject to interest rate changes
(c) they are subject to frequent review as overdrafts are short-term finance
(d) security is usually required
(e) they are repayable on demand.

Example

A firework manufacturer, having a seasonal business, finds that for a period of three months in every year his borrowing requirements exceed the cash he has available. Arrangements are made for an overdraft facility to cover the relevant period. Loan finance is considered inappropriate as money is held on deposit for the rest of the year.

Performance-related contracts

Money may be advanced to an entrepreneur to help him finance activities in pursuance of a contract. This is common in many industries including those involved with research and development, the entertainment industry and authorship. Infrastructure and building projects may also have contracts which are performance-related.

The contract will be policed by the contractor to ensure that the desired outcomes are at least attempted. A contractor's records of performance become an important part of the contract file. Rejections, late deliveries, and other failures of performance will be noted by other contracting officers as they review performance records to determine the responsibility and eligibility of firms for future contracts. The contractee will have the satisfaction of knowing that, should he or she be successful, orders or royalties will be obtained.

Advantages

Advantages of performance-related contracts include:

(a) money is obtained at early stages of the contract, often by way of an advance

(b) there are minimal collateral requirements

(c) definite outcomes, whilst to be attempted, may not be insisted upon owing to certain final outcomes.

Disadvantages

Disadvantages of performance-related contracts include:

(a) the project will be strictly monitored

(b) non-performance may trigger penalty clauses or clawback

(c) the contractee may not have freedom to use end products at his or her own discretion

(d) costly legal fees may be necessary to protect both parties against any future disagreement upon the success or failure of the project.

Example

An author is awarded a contract to write a book of 400 pages, on a given title, within a period of six months. On signing the contract an advance of £1,000 is paid against royalties and on submission of the completed text a further sum of £1,000 is paid. During the course of the contract the author has to submit copies of draft text to the publisher. After publication royalties are paid to the author, less the advances.

The advances provide finance against the cost of writing. In return for this the publishers require constant updates on the work being written.

Retained profits

Retained profits or *general reserves* (see REVENUE RESERVES) are a prime method used to finance business expansion.

The advantages and disadvantages of using retained profits are similar to that of a CASH INPUT except that this money is taken directly from the business rather than from an individual investor. Use of retained profits, by implication, shows that the business is at a stage of maturity where it can consider expansion.

The reserves of a business are a form of collateral that will be noted by financiers, co-investors or suppliers. Using them will show a degree of confidence to grantors or lenders in that the proprietors are willing to risk their own money.

Example

A profitable business is reaching the end of its lease. A freehold site is found that will not only provide ample space for expansion but, if purchased, could also be used as collateral. Finance for the freehold is greater than the cash resources of the business. However, the company's bankers agree to advance a mortgage on the building, which is to be used as security, providing the company uses a substantial proportion of its reserves for the same purpose.

Sale and leaseback

Sale and leaseback involves the sale of a major asset of a business, usually property, to raise finance. The purchaser, obtaining the freehold, will also grant the former owner a lease on the asset. Often, sale and leaseback agreements are arranged between a company and the holders of its pension scheme. The pension fund may be either independent of the business or for a business in which there are many employees within a company pension scheme. Should this method of finance be chosen, the building will become the asset of the pension fund and the business will have to undertake to pay rent and honour other liabilities to the pension scheme. The arrangement must be at arm's length and is therefore unavailable to small owner-run businesses or for companies where there are few employees in the company pension scheme. Protection of pension scheme members is paramount, and mortgage protection policies will be required.

This method of finance is available only to established companies with good quality property or other assets, with values in excess of £500,000.

Advantages:

Advantages of sale and leaseback include:

(a) the vendor will obtain 100% of a property's market value

(b) the property, if sold to a company's pension scheme, will be used as an asset to the benefit of the members

(c) use of the property is retained.

Disadvantages

Disadvantages of sale and leaseback include:

(a) rent will need to be paid, usually increased on review

(b) if the property is sold to a pension scheme it must be at arm's length, and the lease agreement strictly enforced

(c) the agreement cannot be revoked

(d) the asset can no longer be used as collateral

(e) the owner loses title and becomes a tenant

(f) the arrangement is not generally available to small or new businesses.

Share issue

One method by which a limited company may wish to raise finance is through the issue of shares. Generally, shares will normally be issued to existing shareholders in the proportion that they already hold, but this right can be waived so as to allow new shareholders to come into the company. The nominal value of shares would not necessarily reflect the total raised as the shares could be issued for an amount in excess of their nominal value.

Example

A manufacturer of small tools wishes to raise capital for his business. A close friend suggests that he would like to invest in the business. The company already has in issue 8,000 shares with a nominal value of £8,000. An additional 2,000 shares are issued to the friend who pays £10,000 for them. He now owns 20% of the shares in issue whilst the other shareholders' holdings have diminished from 100% to 80%.

Advantages:

Advantages of share issues include:

(a) they provide permanent capital
(b) they are non-interest bearing
(c) they may be cheap to raise.

Disadvantages:

Disadvantages of share issues include:

(a) they dissipate equity in the company
(b) they may be costly to set up
(c) existing shareholders' dividends may be diminished.

Venture capital and the Alternative Investment Market

Venture capital may be defined as equity risk finance offered to unquoted companies with high growth potential. It may be offered at various stages of a company's life including:

(a) **Seed, start-up or early stage**, for example, to fund a new project which has a strong chance of succeeding commercially.

(b) **Development/expansion**, used by established companies to help them to expand, by providing finance to (for example) develop new products and services, buy new plant, or to help them expand a business through acquisition.

(c) **Management buy-in**, whereby outside managers purchase a business.

(d) **Management buy-outs**, whereby current management acquires the business from its parent.

The venture capital investor will acquire an agreed proportion of the business equity. This will often be a minority stake. The aim of the venture capital investor will be to increase the total value to the company's owners without taking control.

Venture capital is risk finance with the investors sharing in the successes or failure of a business like other shareholders. However, venture capital will not be invested unless there is an extremely good likelihood of the business's financial growth and success.

Providers of venture capital

There are different types of venture capital sources, ranging from private investors (business angels) to venture capital firms and they have different investment preferences depending on the business, the industry or stage of development. Publications and information on venture capital can be obtained, generally at no cost, from British Venture Capital Association,

Essex House, 12–13 Essex Street, London WC2R 3AA. Tel: 0171 240 3846; Fax: 0171 240 3849; Web site: http://www.brainstorm.co.uk/bvca.

Advantages

Advantages of venture capital include:

(a) management continue to run their business

(b) expertise from the venture capital investors may be given

(c) venture capital is equity funding. Generally, the principal return to the investor is achieved through the sale of their holding or the flotation of the company

(d) the venture capital investor, as a shareholder, has the same motivation as the proposer and other shareholders in making the company succeed

(e) the venture capital shareholder's motivation is not based upon receipt of interest or dividends, but upon a profit through the sale of equity

(f) venture capital investors will generally need to sell their shares to realise a capital gain. Management will need to buy back these shares. Alternatively, they may wish to sell the company to another, or float on a stock exchange, thereby making more money for themselves

(g) venture capital investors are unlikely to charge their lending policies so their debt is not generally based upon the provision of collateral but upon adequate return on the risk taken.

Disadvantages

Disadvantages of venture capital include:

(a) it is expensive to set up

(b) it is unlikely to be given unless there is a very strong possibility for a successful outcome

(c) management will be answerable to investors.

The Alternative Investment Market (AIM)

AIM is operated by the London Stock Exchange. It provides a means of raising finance, appropriate for young, fast-growing businesses or highly profitable businesses with a good track record that are seeking to expand.

PART 3
Model business plan

Contents

Note to Readers

The publishers are grateful to Hereward Philips, Chartered Accountants, of Whetstone, London, for their assistance and cooperation in reproducing the following specimen business plan.

This sample financial proposal is the result of working closely with a wide variety of clients over many years and is based on feedback and suggestions obtained from banks, other lenders and investors.

The publishers wish to emphasise that this example may not be suitable in all cases and readers are strongly advised NOT to follow its format slavishly.

This sample financial proposal has been prepared using *fictitious* names and financial information and any similarity between the contents of this document and any real company or business organisation is entirely coincidental.

Super Systems Limited – Financing proposal

1. Introduction

Super Systems Limited was incorporated on 1 June 1997.

The company is currently based at Unit 7, South Industrial Estate, North Road, Bradford-on-Avon, Wiltshire and plans to operate from Whetstone, London, when trading.

The principal activity of the company will be to import and distribute accounting systems manufactured by Schmidt GmbH, a West Germany company.

It is intended that the company will commence trading on 1 January 1998.

The projected results for the first two years are as follows:

Year ended 31 December	1998		1999	
	£000s		£000s	
Turnover	993		1,200	
	====		====	
Gross profit	174	17.6%	262	21.9%
	====		====	
Net profit before taxation	25		89	
	====		====	
Maximum overdraft	96		34	
	====		====	
Arising in:	June 1998		June 1999	

Detailed schedules relating to the financial projects for Year 1, the year ended 31 December 1998, are included in Appendix C. Workings relating to the second year of trading are not included but are available for inspection.

The directors and shareholders (50% holding each) are Roger Smith (Managing Director) and David Jones (Marketing Director).

2. Funding requirements

The company requires finance of £105,000 by way of an overdraft facility.

The directors propose to contribute £50,000 personally to finance initial trading losses and capital additions.

3. Details of the business

The product

The company has negotiated an agreement to act as sole UK distributor for the products of Schmidt GmbH, which produces accounting systems for manufacturing companies.

The accounting systems have been widely used in Western Europe since 1991 and sell under the name of 'ACCPRO'. So far, ACCPRO has been available in the UK through local agents only.

Although the product has consistently been given favourable reviews in the trade press, the market for Schmidt's systems has not been developed to its full potential in the UK through the lack of an effective marketing and distribution network.

The current list price of ACCPRO is £5,000 per unit. However, as is the case throughout the market, discounts will be given with large orders.

The cost of ACCPRO has been fixed by a distribution agreement for an initial term of five years with an option to renegotiate every two years.

During the first two years of the agreement, ACCPRO will be purchased at £3,800 including all freight and import charges to be invoiced in sterling.

The agreement allows for variations in price of up to 7.5% in either direction to allow for significant changes in production costs. Schmidt is required to give three months notice of any changes in price.

Marketing and sales projection

For the past two months both directors have been following up numerous contacts from their previous employments and in total have seen and arranged product demonstrations for 50 potential customers. In addition they have obtained over 30 valuable leads from the Accountants Exhibition at which they held a stand in July 1997.

The sales projection for the first year of trading is based on both specific known orders and upon the directors' estimates of smaller orders as a result of their marketing efforts so far.

The directors have conducted negotiations with a number of major companies and have secured advance orders during the first year of trading to the value of £472,500, analysed as follows:

	Units	£
Major Plc	60	270,000
Blue Chip Plc	30	135,000
Multinational Plc	15	67,500
	105	472,500

Copies of provisional orders from these companies are enclosed in Appendix B.

The specific advance orders as detailed above will be at a discounted price of £4,500. Other sales will be made at the full price of £5,000.

Based on the past performance of the product in the UK, the pattern of sales is not thought to be significantly affected by seasonal factors.

The directors are confident that sales volumes will be maintained in the second year of trading. This excludes any specific large orders such as those achieved in Year 1.

The overall market for accounting systems such as ACCPRO is expanding rapidly. The total market was valued at £25 million in the year to March 1995. The market is projected to grow at an annual rate of 10% until 1998. The directors' sales projection represents approximately 4% of the total UK market over the next two years.

The two largest participants in the accounting systems market, ABC plc and XYZ plc, together take a 55% market share. However the majority of the expansion in sales in the past two years has been in medium-sized systems, such as ACCPRO. ABC and XYZ do not dominate this sector of the market and concentrate on larger systems.

Super Systems will be in direct competition with approximately 20 similar sized organisations. The main advantage that the company has over these competitors is that it can remain relatively small whilst selling a product manufactured by a substantial European company.

Location

The company will operate from a leasehold industrial unit in Whetstone, London.

Details of premises:

Size	5,000 sq ft
Description:	Warehouse and office accommodation (70/30)
Rateable value:	£3,500
Duration of lease:	20 years
Annual rental:	£25,500
Rent reviews:	five yearly – Next review due 30/08/2002
Freeholders:	Sun Insurance Co. Limited

4. Participants, management and other personnel

The issued share capital of the company will be divided equally between the two directors, Roger Smith and David Jones.

Both the directors have sufficient personal assets to enable them to finance their capital injections personally.

It has been agreed that Roger Smith will be appointed Managing Director and David Jones will be appointed Marketing Director.

A detailed curriculum vitae for each director is included under Appendix A.

At the anticipated level of turnover in the first two years of trading, all management expertise will be provided by the two directors. Both directors will be primarily engaged in selling although Roger Smith will take direct responsibility for administration.

The directors have specifically identified the need for additional help in the following areas:

(a) The maintenance of accounting records and credit control.
A full time bookkeeper/secretary will be employed to assist the directors in the above.

(b) The maintenance and development of financial controls.

It is proposed that the company's auditors and accountants will assist with:

  (i) the preparation of periodic management accounts
 (ii) the preparation of budgets and cashflow forecasts
(iii) the development and improvement of internal controls to assist management as the company grows

(iv) the provision of general financial advice based on formal periodic management meetings.

Staff projected as required and their related costs are as follows:

Year ended 31 December:	1998	1999
	£	£
Directors' remuneration	34,992	45,832
Bookkeeper/Secretary	9,000	9,500
Warehouse	19,992	21,492
National Insurance	6,672	8,022
	70,656	84,846

In addition to the above basic pay pension contributions will be paid as follows:

Directors	4,200	4,200

It is not envisaged that any additional staff will be required in the first two years.

5. Financial information

Projected profit and loss accounts and balance sheets

The company's projected results for the first two years are as follows:

(a) Profit and loss accounts	Year ended 31/12/98 £000s		Year Ended 31/12/99 £000s	
Sales – units	209		240	
	====		====	
Turnover	£000s		£000s	
	993		1,200	
	====		====	
Gross profit	174	17.6%	262	21.9%
	====		====	
Accommodation	42		49	
Administration	25		27	
Selling and distribution	37		42	
Directors' remuneration	43		55	
	147		173	
	====		====	
Net profit before interest	27		89	
Interest	2			
Net profit before tax	25		89	
	====		====	

(b) Balance sheets	31/12/98	31/12/99
	£000s	£000s
Fixed assets	12	8
	====	====
Net current assets		
Stock	95	57
Trade debtors	182	162
Bank current account	(26)	72
Trade creditors	(174)	(137)
VAT control	(17)	(7)
PAYE creditor	(2)	(3)
Corporation tax	(6)	(22)
Sundry accruals and prepayments	5	5
	57	127
	====	====
Net assets	69	135
	====	====
Capital and reserves:		
Called up share capital	50	50
Profit and loss account	19	85
	69	135
	===	====

The projected trading results in the first year show a lower gross profit percentage as a result of three large orders at a discounted selling price.

No allowance for discounted prices has been made in the second year as it has been assumed that the projected sales will be achieved from smaller orders at full list price.

Sensitivity analysis

The directors have identified both the level of turnover and the purchase price as critical factors.

The anticipated effect of these factors on both profitability and on the maximum overdraft requirement for the first year of trading is shown on the graphs in Appendices C9 and C10.

Assuming that all other factors remain constant, the sensitivity of overdraft and profit to budgeted sales shows that:

(a) the break-even point occurs at approximately 86% of budgeted sales

(b) were the company to achieve 70% of budgeted sales a loss of approximately £28,000 is projected

(c) the overdraft requirement would be approximately £88,000 at break-even which would also occur in June 1998.

(d) over the range between 70% and 100% of budgeted sales the maximum overdraft is projected to vary approximately between £79,000 and £96,000 respectively. Once again June is the month in which any maximum overdraft would be required.

June is likely to be the month in which the maximum overdraft occurs in Year 1 for the following reasons:

(i) Payments to Schmidt GmbH for systems sold in May, the first month in which sales of significant value are projected, will be made in June in full whereas only 50% of May sales are projected to be received by the end of June. As takings increase in July, the projected overdraft dips significantly in this month.

(ii) The VAT liability for the quarter to 31 May is payable by the end of June and the quarterly rent charge also falls due in June.

The cashflow imbalance described in (i) is therefore enhanced by the cashflow timings described in (ii).

However, as projected activity is reduced so is the overall working capital requirement and so the projected maximum overdraft is also reduced.

Assuming that all other factors remain constant, the sensitivity of overdraft and profit to budgeted purchase price shows that:

(a) the break-even point occurs at approximately 103% of budgeted purchase price

(b) were the suppliers to increase their prices by the maximum possible of

7.5% (see Details of the business, The product, p.140), a loss of approximately £37,000 is projected, assuming that these increases are not passed on to customers.

Projected cashflow statements

The sources and applications of funds giving rise to the projected bank overdrafts for the first six months (to maximum overdraft) and the first complete year are summarised as follows:

	01/01/98 to 30/06/98 (Maximum overdraft)		01/01/98 to 31/12/98	
Sources of funds	£000s		£000s	
Profit/(loss) before taxation	(28)		25	
Depreciation	2		3	
Share capital introduced	50		50	
		24		78
Application of funds				
Purchase of fixed assets		(15)		(15)
Increases in working capital:				
Stock	(156)		(95)	
Trade debtors	(245)		(182)	
Trade creditors	278		174	
Other debtors/creditors	18		14	
		(105)		(89)
Increase in bank overdraft		(96)		(26)
		====		====

It is clear from the above analysis that the share capital to be introduced will finance both fixed asset purchases and the losses incurred during the first four months of the year.

Working capital requirements of approximately £105,000 during the first six months of trading are to be funded by an overdraft facility together with the remainder of the capital injection.

The cashflow projections show a maximum overdraft in the first year of £95,653. After allowing a margin of safety an overdraft facility of £105,000 will be required.

147

In the second year the maximum overdraft is projected as approximately £34,000 in June. This is on the assumption that sales will follow a similar seasonal variation as in Year 1.

Should any particularly large orders be secured in Year 2, a higher overdraft than is shown in the projection may result. With this in mind an overdraft facility of £60,000 in Year 2 will be required to allow sufficient working capital to finance larger orders, should they arise.

Fixed assets

The fixed assets to be acquired are as follows:

	£
Fork-lift truck	3,000
Warehouse racking and equipment	5,000
Computer and printer	3,000
Other office equipment and fittings	4,000
	15,000

Two motor cars for use by the directors will be financed by an operating lease.

Appendix A
Directors' curriculum vitae

Appendix A1 Roger Smith

Curriculum Vitae – Roger Smith

Address: 31 Crescent Avenue
                     Whetstone
                     London N20

Date of birth: 30/06/48

Marital status: Married, two children.

Health: Excellent. Non-smoker.

Education: Graduated from Middlesex Polytechnic (now University of Middlesex) in 1969 with an Honours degree in Business Studies.

Career history: After graduation took up a position as management trainee with Systems UK.

                     1980 – Reached the position of Chief Sales Co-ordinator.

                     1984 – Joined Agents Limited and was responsible for that company's role as agents for Schmidt products in the UK.

                     In the past two years Roger Smith has increasingly been aware of the rising demand for Schmidt products in the UK. It has become clear that this demand cannot be fully satisfied under the existing agency agreement.

                     After substantial negotiations, Schmidt GmbH has recently accepted the proposal for setting up a UK company to act as sole distributor for its accounting systems.

Roger Smith has informed Agents Limited of his plans and they part on amicable terms. He is not subject to any restrictive covenants with his present company.

Personal assets	Freehold interest in private house	£
	Market value	180,000
	Mortgage secured on property	(60,000)
		————
	Net equity in property	120,000
	Value of shares in listed company (net of CGT liability)	50,000
		————
		170,000
		======

Description of Property	Four-bedroom semi-detached, double garage, 20 years old.
Mortgagee:	Whetstone Building Society
Personal bankers:	Clearers Plc, High Street, Whetstone.

Appendix A2 David Jones

Curriculum Vitae – David Jones

Address:	17 Brookfield Avenue Whetstone London N20
Date of birth:	17/02/57
Marital status:	Married, one child.
Health:	Excellent. Non-smoker.
Education:	Graduated from Liverpool University in 1978 with a First Class Honours degree in Marketing.
Career History:	1979 – Joined Advertisers UK Limited where he received further training in marketing.

Reached the position of Account Manager in 1981.

1983 – Left Advertisers UK Limited to work for the international company Worldwide Advertisers Plc. Appointed to the position of Marketing Director in 1987.

Since 1987 Worldwide Advertisers plc has handled marketing and promotion of Schmidt products in the UK on behalf of Agents Ltd. David Jones has been directly responsible for this account since that time. Following an internal reorganisation at Worldwide, David Jones decided to accept voluntary redundancy.

Personal assets:	Freehold interest in private house	£
	Market value	120,000
	Mortgage secured on property	(33,000)
		———
	Net equity in property	87,000
	Cash on deposit in building societies	34,000
		———
		121,000
		======

Description of property:	Three-bedroom semi-detached, single garage 30 years old.
Mortgagee:	Bank of Wales
Personal bankers:	Clearers Plc, High Street, Whetstone.

Appendix B – Copies of orders

Appendix B1

Major Plc

137 West End Street • Newtown • Beds

D. Jones, Esq.
Super Systems Limited
Unit 7, South Industrial Estate
North Road
Bradford-on-Avon
Wiltshire

29 July 1997

Dear Mr Jones

Further to our recent meeting between ourselves and your colleague Mr Smith, I confirm my company's provisional order for 60 units of your accounting system.

As agreed the order is for delivery in monthly batches of 20 units commencing May 1998.

The agreed price per unit is £4,500.

Yours sincerely

E.R. Brown
Chief Buyer

Registered in England No. [number]. Registered Office: [detail].

Appendix B2

Blue Chip plc

190 East End Street
Old Town
Bucks

The Directors
Super Systems Limited
Unit 7, South Industrial Estate
North Road
Bradford-on-Avon
Wiltshire   3 July 1997

Dear Sirs

As discussed at our recent meeting I confirm our order for 30 units of your company's accounting systems at a unit price of £4,500.

We shall expect delivery to commence in January 1998 and shall provide formal works orders for each shipment.

Yours faithfully

A.S. Green

Production Manager

Registered in England No. [number]. Registered Office: [detail].

Appendix B3

MULTINATIONAL PLC

1021 City Road

London

The Directors,
Super Systems Limited,
Unit 7, South Industrial Estate,
North Road,
Bradford-on-Avon,
Wiltshire,

3 September 1997

Dear Sirs,

I confirm my company's order for 15 units of Super Systems' accounting systems at a unit price of £4,500.

Please arrange for delivery commencing May 1998.

Yours faithfully,

W.E. Black

Purchasing Manager

Registered in England No. [number]. Registered Office: [detail].

Appendix C – Financial projections

Appendix C1 Assumptions

1. Cash will be received from invoiced sales according to the following pattern:

After 30 days	50%
After 60 days	50%

2. Under the agreement made with Schmidt, purchases will be paid for 60 days after delivery.

3. Other credit purchases will be paid according to the following pattern:

0 to 30 days	10%
After 30 days	30%
After 60 days	40%
After 90 days	20%

4. Carriage and freight outward has been estimated at 2% of invoiced sales.

5. Sufficient stock of accounting systems will be held to satisfy anticipated sales in the following month.

6. PAYE and employees' and employers' National Insurance will amount to 40% of total gross salaries.

7. Overdraft interest has been calculated based on the average monthly current account balance at an annual rate of 10%.

8. Legal and professional fees covering the negotiation of the agreement with Schmidt will amount to £1,000.

9. The provision for corporation tax has been based on the account's profit using existing corporation tax rates.

10. No provision has been made for bad debts.

11. Allowance for inflationary increases in overheads has been made in Year 2.

Appendix C2 Accounting policies

1. The projections have been prepared under the historical cost convention.

2. Stock has been valued at cost.

3. Depreciation has been provided on fixed assets at the following annual rates:

Office equipment	20%
Warehouse equipment	20%
Fork-lift truck	25%
Computer and printer	25%

APPENDIX C3 Cashflow forecast (1)

Super Systems Limited Cashflow Forecast (1)
Year ended 31 December 1998

	JAN	FEB	MAR	APR	MAY	JUN	JUL	AUG	SEP	OCT	NOV	DEC	TOTAL
Receipts													
Sales ledger				5,875	17,625	89,593	161,561	193,874	165,968	111,624	114,562	123,375	984,057
Interest receivable													
Share capital	50,000												50,000
Bad debts													
	50,000			5,875	17,625	89,593	161,561	193,874	165,968	111,624	114,562	123,375	1,034,057
Opening bank balance	50,000	20,051	12,249	(2,904)	(15,270)	(27,321)	(95,756)	(66,996)	(42,228)	(44,561)	(21,590)	4,151	
Receipts	50,000			5,875	17,625	89,593	161,561	193,874	165,968	111,624	114,562	123,375	1,034,057
Payments	(29,949)	(7,802)	(15,153)	(18,241)	(29,676)	(158,028)	(132,801)	(169,106)	(168,301)	(88,683)	(88,821)	(153,840)	(1,060,371)
Closing bank balance	20,051	12,249	(2,904)	(15,270)	(27,321)	(95,756)	(66,996)	(42,228)	(44,561)	(21,590)	4,151	(26,314)	(26,314)

MAXIMUM

Maximum overdraft: 95,756 ======

Minimum in hand: ======

APPENDIX C4 Cashflow forecast (2)

Super Systems Limited Cashflow Forecast (2)
Year ended 31 December 1998

	JAN	FEB	MAR	APR	MAY	JUN	JUL	AUG	SEP	OCT	NOV	DEC	TOTAL
PAYMENTS													
VATable items:													
Carriage and freight			235	470	3,113	3,348	4,406	2,232	2,232	2,350	2,585	2,350	23,321
Sundry	200	200	200	200	200	200	200	200	200	200	200	200	2,400
Computer equipment	3,000												3,000
Office equipment	4,000												4,000
Warehouse equipment	5,000												5,000
Fork lift truck	3,000												3,000
Lease of cars	1,620	540	540	540	540	540	540	540	540	540	540	540	7,560
	16,820	740	975	1,210	3,853	4,088	5,146	2,972	2,972	3,090	3,325	3,090	48,281
VAT 17.5%	2,943	129	170	211	674	715	900	520	520	540	581	540	8,443
Non-VATable items:													
Rent	6,375		6,375			6,375			6,375			6,375	31,875
Rates and water			2,250	750	750	750	750	750	750	750	750	750	9,000
Service charge		150			150			150			150		600
Purchases ledger				7,600	15,200	110,200	117,800	155,800	76,000	76,000	76,000	83,600	718,200
Expense ledger	278	895	1,752	2,232	2,211	1,848	1,967	2,676	2,449	2,035	1,777	1,315	21,435
Directors' pension costs			1,050	350	350	350	350	350	350	350	350	350	4,200
Directors' medical insurance					600								600
Net wages	3,533	3,533	3,533	3,533	3,533	3,533	3,533	3,533	3,533	3,533	3,533	3,533	42,396
PAYE-current		2,355	2,355	2,355	2,355	2,355	2,355	2,355	2,355	2,355	2,355	2,355	25,905
Loan repayments													
Bank charges			200			200			200			200	800
Bank interest						764			1,494			439	2,697
Payments to C & E			(3,507)			26,850			71,303			51,293	145,939
Directors loan account													
	29,949	7,802	15,153	18,241	29,676	158,028	132,801	169,106	168,301	88,653	88,821	153,840	1,060,371

APPENDIX C5 Forecast profit and loss account

Super Systems Limited Forecast Profit and Loss Account
Year ended 31 December 1998

	JAN	FEB	MAR	APR	MAY	JUN	JUL	AUG	SEP	OCT	NOV	DEC	TOTAL	Projected Year Ended 31.12.97
Turnover			10,000	20,000	132,500	142,500	187,500	95,000	95,000	100,000	110,000	100,000	992,500	1,200,000
Cost of sales	1,985	1,985	9,585	17,185	112,185	119,785	157,785	77,985	77,985	77,985	85,585	77,985	818,020	937,480
Gross profit	(1,985)	(1,985)	415	2,815	20,315	22,715	29,715	17,015	17,015	22,015	24,415	22,015	174,480	262,520
Accommodation	3,545	3,545	3,545	3,545	3,545	3,545	3,545	3,545	3,545	3,545	3,545	3,555	42,550	48,520
Administration	2,046	2,046	2,046	2,046	2,046	2,046	2,046	2,046	2,046	2,046	2,046	2,066	24,572	27,122
Selling and distribution	1,101	1,101	1,336	1,571	4,214	4,449	5,507	3,333	3,333	3,451	3,686	3,469	36,551	42,137
Directors' remuneration	3,620	3,620	3,620	3,620	3,620	3,620	3,620	3,620	3,620	3,620	3,620	3,620	43,440	55,480
	10,312	10,312	10,547	10,782	13,425	13,660	14,718	12,544	12,544	12,662	12,897	12,710	147,113	173,259
	(12,297)	(12,297)	(10,132)	(7,967)	6,890	9,055	14,997	4,471	4,471	9,353	11,518	9,305	27,367	89,261
Interest receivable														1,044
Interest payable				(75)	(177)	(512)	(678)	(455)	(361)	(275)	(72)	(92)	(2,697)	(1,272)
Profit on ordinary activities before taxation	(12,297)	(12,297)	(10,132)	(8,042)	6,713	8,543	14,319	4,016	4,110	9,078	11,446	9,213	24,670	89,033
Taxation	(3,074)	(3,074)	(2,532)	(2,010)	1,678	2,135	3,579	1,003	1,027	2,269	2,861	2,305	6,167	22,258
Profit on ordinary activities after taxation	(9,223)	(9,223)	(7,600)	(6,032)	5,035	6,408	10,740	3,013	3,083	6,809	8,585	6,908	18,503	66,775
Dividend														
Surplus brought forward		(9,223)	(18,446)	(26,046)	(32,078)	(27,043)	(20,635)	(9,895)	(6,882)	(3,799)	3,010	11,595		18,503
Surplus carried forward	(9,223)	(18,446)	(26,046)	(32,078)	(27,043)	(20,635)	(9,895)	(6,882)	(3,799)	3,010	11,595	18,503	18,503	85,278

APPENDIX C6 Detail of forecast profit and loss account (1)

Super Systems Limited Detail of Forecast Profit and Loss Account (1)
Year ended 31 December 1998

	JAN	FEB	MAR	APR	MAY	JUN	JUL	AUG	SEP	OCT	NOV	DEC	TOTAL	Projected Year Ended 31.12.98
Sales			10,000	20,000	132,500	142,500	187,500	95,000	95,000	100,000	110,000	100,000	992,500	1,200,000
Cost of sales														
Opening stocks			7,600	15,200	110,200	117,800	155,800	76,000	76,000	76,000	83,600	76,000		95,000
Purchases		7,600	15,200	110,200	117,800	155,800	76,000	76,000	76,000	83,600	76,000	95,000	889,200	874,000
Direct wages and staff costs	1,840	1,840	1,840	1,840	1,840	1,840	1,840	1,840	1,840	1,840	1,840	1,840	22,080	23,740
Depreciation of warehouse equipment	83	83	83	83	83	83	83	83	83	83	83	83	996	996
Depreciation of fork lift truck	62	62	62	62	62	62	62	62	62	62	62	62	744	744
	1,985	9,585	24,785	127,385	229,985	275,585	233,785	153,985	153,985	161,585	161,585	172,985	913,020	994,480
Closing stocks		7,600	15,200	110,200	117,800	155,800	76,000	76,000	76,000	83,600	76,000	95,000	95,000	57,000
	1,985	1,985	9,585	17,185	112,185	119,785	157,785	77,985	77,015	77,985	85,585	77,985	818,020	937,480
Gross profit	(1,985)	(1,985)	415	2,815	20,315	22,715	29,715	17,015	17,015	22,015	24,415	22,015	174,480	262,520
	4.15%	4.15%	4.15%	14.08%	15.33%	15.94%	15.85%	17.91%	17.91%	22.02%	22.02%	22.02%	17.58%	21.88%
Accommodation														
Rent	2,125	2,125	2,125	2,125	2,125	2,125	2,125	2,125	2,125	2,125	2,125	2,125	25,500	31,875
Rates and water	750	750	750	750	750	750	750	750	750	750	750	750	9,000	9,450
Service charge	50	50	50	50	50	50	50	50	50	50	50	50	600	775
Light and heat	225	225	225	225	225	225	225	225	225	225	225	225	2,700	2,970
Insurance	125	125	125	125	125	125	125	125	125	125	125	125	1,500	1,800
Repairs to premises	270	270	270	270	270	270	270	270	270	270	270	280	3,250	1,650
	3,545	3,545	3,545	3,545	3,545	3,545	3,545	3,545	3,545	3,545	3,545	3,555	42,550	48,520

APPENDIX C7 *Detail of forecast profit and loss account (2)*

Super Systems Limited Detail of Forecast Profit and Loss Account (2)
Year ended 31 December 1998

	JAN	FEB	MAR	APR	MAY	JUN	JUL	AUG	SEP	OCT	NOV	DEC	TOTAL	Projected Year Ended 31.12.97
Administration														
Telephone	383	383	383	383	383	383	383	383	383	383	383	387	4,600	4,800
Printing, postage and stationery	108	108	108	108	108	108	108	108	108	108	108	112	1,300	1,860
Secretary/bookkeeper	828	828	828	828	828	828	828	828	828	828	828	828	9,936	10,486
Audit and accountancy	250	250	250	250	250	250	250	250	250	250	250	250	3,000	4,000
Legal and professional	83	83	83	83	83	83	83	83	83	83	83	87	800	1,000
Bank charges	66	66	66	66	66	66	66	66	66	66	66	74	800	800
Sundry expenses	200	200	200	200	200	200	200	200	200	200	200	200	2,400	2,640
Depreciation of computer	62	62	62	62	62	62	62	62	62	62	62	62	744	744
Depreciation of office equipment	66	66	66	66	66	66	66	66	66	66	66	66	792	792
	2,046	2,046	2,046	2,046	2,046	2,046	2,046	2,046	2,046	2,046	2,046	2,066	24,572	27,122
Selling and Distribution														
Carriage and freight			235	470	3,113	3,348	4,406	2,232	2,232	2,350	2,585	2,350	23,321	28,197
Advertising	166	166	166	166	166	166	166	166	166	166	166	174	2,000	2,200
Lease of cars	540	540	540	540	540	5440	540	540	540	540	540	540	6,480	6,480
Motor and travel	395	395	395	395	395	395	395	395	395	395	395	405	4,750	5,260
Bad debts	0	0	0	0	0	0	0	0	0	0	0	0	0	0
	1,101	1,101	1,336	1,571	4,214	4,449	5,507	3,333	3,333	3,451	3,686	3,469	36,551	42,137
Directors' Remuneration														
Salaries	2,916	2,916	2,916	2,916	2,916	2,916	2,916	2,916	2,916	2,916	2,916	2,916	34,992	45,832
National Insurance	304	304	304	304	304	304	304	304	304	304	304	304	3,648	4,788
Pension	350	350	350	350	350	350	350	350	350	350	350	350	4,200	4,200
Directors' medical insurance	50	50	50	50	50	50	50	50	50	50	50	50	600	660
	3,620	3,620	3,620	3,620	3,620	3,620	3,620	3,620	3,620	3,620	3,620	3,620	43,440	55,480
Interest payable														
Bank interest				75	177	512	678	455	361	275	72	92	2,697	1,272
Bank loan interest				75	177	512	678	455	361	275	72	92	2,697	1,272

APPENDIX C8 Forecast balance sheet

Super Systems Limited Balance Sheet
Year ended 31 December 1997

	JAN	FEB	MAR	APR	MAY	JUN	JUL	AUG	SEP	OCT	NOV	DEC	Projected Year Ended 31.12.97
Fixed assets													
Tangible Assets	14,727	14,454	14,181	13,908	13,635	13,362	13,089	12,816	12,543	12,270	11,997	11,724	8,448
Current assets													
Stock		7,600	15,200	110,200	117,800	155,800	76,000	76,000	76,000	83,600	76,000	95,000	57,000
Trade debtors			11,750	29,375	167,437	245,281	304,032	221,783	167,440	173,316	188,004	182,129	161,574
Cash	20,051	12,249											
Bank	(2,507)	(9,812)	(2,904)	(15,270)	(27,321)	(95,756)	(66,996)	(42,228)	(44,561)	(21,590)	4,151	(26,314)	71,679
Business reserve													
Trade creditors	3,303	3,507	(27,845)	(128,813)	(229,974)	(278,333)	(236,143)	(155,744)	(156,047)	(162,269)	(161,149)	(174,301)	(136,588)
VAT creditor	(2,355)	(2,355)	(1,220)	(4,434)	(26,850)	(23,690)	(55,400)	(71,303)	(15,828)	(32,706)	(51,293)	(16,668)	(6,777)
PAYE creditor			(2,355)	(2,355)	(2,355)	(2,355)	(2,355)	(2,355)	(2,355)	(2,355)	(2,355)	(2,355)	(2,922)
Bank loan													
Directors loan													
Corporation tax	3,074	6,148	8,680	10,690	9,012	6,877	3,298	2,295	1,268	(1,001)	(3,862)	(6,167)	(22,302)
Accruals and prepayments	4,484	(237)	8,467	4,621	1,573	8,179	4,580	1,854	7,741	3,745	102	5,455	5,176
	26,050	17,100	9,773	4,014	9,322	16,003	27,016	30,302	33,658	40,740	49,598	56,779	126,840
Total assets less current liabilities	40,777	31,554	23,954	17,992	22,957	29,365	40,105	43,118	46,201	53,010	61,595	68,503	135,278
Creditors due after one year													
Bank loan													
	40,777	31,554	23,954	17,922	22,957	29,365	40,105	43,118	46,201	53,010	61,595	68,503	135,278
Capital and reserves													
Called up share capital	50,000	50,000	50,000	50,000	50,000	50,000	50,000	50,000	50,000	50,010	50,000	50,000	50,000
Profit and loss account	(9,223)	(18,446)	(26,046)	(32,078)	(27,043)	(20,635)	(9,895)	(6,882)	(3,799)	3,010	11,595	18,503	85,278
	40,777	31,554	23,954	17,922	22,957	29,365	40,105	43,118	46,201	53,010	61,595	68,503	135,278

APPENDIX C9 *Sensitivity of overdraft and profit to budgeted sales*

Super Systems Limited
Sensitivity of profit and maximum overdraft to turnover

Profit Before Tax	— ‧ — ‧ — ‧ —
Maximum Overdraft	– – – – – – –

Sensitivity of overdraft and profit to budgeted sales

£'000

150
100
50
0
(50)
(100)

100% 90% 80% 70% 60% 50% 40%

Percentage of turnover

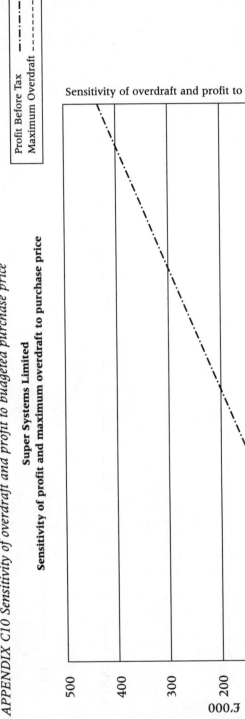

APPENDIX C10 Sensitivity of overdraft and profit to budgeted purchase price

Super Systems Limited

Sensitivity of profit and maximum overdraft to purchase price

Sensitivity of overdraft and profit to budgeted purchase price

Percentage of purchase price

£,000

Profit Before Tax
Maximum Overdraft

Bibliography

Accountants Digest, S. G. Hastie, Accountancy Books
Accounting Made Simple, J. P. Simini an A. J. Grant, W. H. Allen
Analysing Financial Statements, S. Gilman, The Ronald Press Company
Business Opportunity World – Supplement, September 1996
Company Secretary's Factbook, Vol 2, Gee Publishing Ltd
Countertrade and Offset, Overseas Trade Services, March 1996
Essential Facts – Credit Control and Debt Recovery, Gee Publishing Ltd
Export Import, Joseph Zodl, Betterway Books, 1995
Finance Without Debt, DTI, February 1996
Financial Reporting and Disclosure Manual, Gee Publishing Ltd, May 1997
Financial Statement Analysis, Baruch Lev, Prentice Hall
Guide to Factoring and Discounting, DTI, March 1995
Guide to Hire Purchase and Leasing, DTI, March 1995
Guide to Lump Sum Investment. Liz Walkington, Kogan Page
How to Apply for Grants Loans and Other Sources of Finance, Harris Rosenberg,
    Gee Publishing Ltd 1996
A Summary of the Chancellor's Statement, Budget 1996, Hughes Allen
Insight into Management Accounting, J. Sizer, Pelican Books
Introduction to Business Accounting for Managers, W. C. S. Hartley, Pergamon
    International Library
Managing Into the 90s, Market Research, DTI
Members Handbook, Volume II (Accounting), The Institute of Chartered
    Accountants in England and Wales, 1996
Members Handbook, Volume III (Auditing and Reporting), The Institute of
    Chartered Accountants in England and Wales, 1996
Factsheet, Morley & Scott, 1996
One Stop Company Secretary, D. M. Martin, ICSA Publishing
Raising Finance, Barclays Bank – Barclays Net at http://www.barclays.co.uk
Raising Finance, The Guardian Guide for the Small Business, Woodcock,
    Kogan Page
Russia – Market Approaches, David Cant and Harris Rosenberg, Gee
    Publishing Ltd, 1994
Small Business Factbook, Gee Publishing Ltd
Small Firms – Finance Without Debt, DTI, February 1996
Smart Business Supersite at http://www.smartbiz.com

Tax Guide 1996/97 – Sara Williams and John Willman, Lloyds Bank
Understanding Company Financial Statements – R. H. Parker, Pelican Books
Understanding Insolvency, Society of Practitioners of Insolvency